Ready to Fire

To

SAPL
Best of luck
for your
support

R Rickettohns

6/12/85

Ready to Fire

*Memoir of an
American Artilleryman
in the Korean War*

RICHARD B. HOLMSTEN

McFarland & Company, Inc., Publishers
Jefferson, North Carolina, and London

LIBRARY OF CONGRESS CATALOGUING-IN-PUBLICATION DATA

Holmsten, Richard B.
    Ready to fire : memoir of an American artilleryman in the
Korean War / Richard B. Holmsten.
        p.   cm.
    Includes index.

    ISBN 0-7864-1613-0 (softcover : 50# alkaline paper) ∞

    1. Korean War, 1950–1953—Personal narratives, American.
2. Holmsten, Richard B.   3. Soldiers—United States—
Biography.   I. Title.
DS921.6.H65   2003
951.9'042373'092—dc21
                                              2003013579

British Library cataloguing data are available

Cover image: Dick Holmsten in Korea, 1951

Manufactured in the United States of America

McFarland & Company, Inc., Publishers
    Box 611, Jefferson, North Carolina 28640
        www.mcfarlandpub.com

To my wife Florence—
her faith, support and almost daily letters while
I was in Korea made my tour of duty bearable

ACKNOWLEDGMENTS

This historical narrative could not have been completed without the help of many fine people. Florence, my wife, who kept every letter I wrote from Korea, deserves credit for this book. My comrades in arms—Robert Schranck, Sefton Stallard, Joseph Quartararo, Arthur Schwerin, Rodman Scheffer and Robert Baur—were with me during the Korean conflict and they remain an ever-present part of my memory. I must also thank Carleton Vang for his friendship, willingness and skill to help convert my diary to a narrative that tells my story in a readable manner. And to the combined Allied forces which fought in the Korean campaign, my undying gratitude.

TABLE OF CONTENTS

PREFACE

This book starts while I was in the inactive enlisted reserve and still a civilian in Minnesota. The disaster that wiped out the Fire Direction Center on August 22, 1950, set in motion my recall from the reserve and assignment to join the Headquarters Battery of the 8th Field Artillery Battalion of the 25th Infantry Division near Kaesong, Korea, in December of 1950.

The book records my transition from civilian status in Minnesota to that of a newly married young soldier suddenly thrust into the Korean conflict. It is compiled from letters sent to my wife while I was stationed in Korea, and records my activities as I leave home, my personal army experiences in training camp at Fort Lewis, my voyage across the Pacific, my arrival in replacement camp, and my subsequent assignment to Headquarters Battery, 8th Field Artillery Battalion, of the 25th Division.

With the Fire Direction Control Center fully operational, we were moved out of Inchon into the field. From that point on, the book becomes an historical account of how Headquarters Battery 105 Howitzer Fire Direction Unit operated, and what happened during those early days of conflict as the unit moved north and south in the flux and flow of battle. It covers the problems we faced as we retreated through Seoul, and as we regrouped to strike north again. The major campaign in this book concerns the coordination effort that went into the crossing of the Han River in March of 1951. Our Fire Direction Center was the nucleus of the division assault and we were responsible for firing over 7,000 rounds of artillery, making this a fast crossing with light casualties.

This is a story of one man's journey from home, to war, and home again, recorded in letters to his wife, from the time he joined

1

the field command until the time he was rotated back to civilian life. The daily happenings, the situations, the action, the fear, the hope and the disappointments are recounted from the Fire Direction Center in which he worked. The events also introduce many of the men who were assigned to the Headquarters Battery, and what they did as the war progressed.

1

LEAVING

When North Korean troops invaded South Korea by crossing the 38th Parallel on June 25, 1950, I, like most civilians, paid scant attention to the incursion. I was involved in my own world, my own plans, my own problems, and though the invasion was prime-time news, and on everyone's lips, I went about my life thinking I would not be bothered by someone else's war.

On the day of the attack, my fiancée, Florence White, and I were in Kensington, Minnesota, on a beautiful spring day, attending the wedding of the cousin of the man that was to be our best man at the wedding that had not yet been announced. Florence and I had announced our engagement on April 1, 1950, without setting a wedding date. At that point in our lives we seemed to have all the time in the world. She would be starting her senior year at the University of Minnesota and I was working with my father at Holmsten Refrigeration, Inc., as an installer, starting at the bottom to work my way up in the trade. I was unsure if I would return to the University of Minnesota to finish my formal education, or devote myself totally to the firm. The refrigeration business was booming. My future looked rosy. The affair in Kensington, with its flowers and merriment and friendship, was a prelude to the wedding Florence and I would eventually have. It was a beautiful ceremony. Our thoughts were not on war, but on each other, and on a future that extended beyond our imagination.

I was an inactive reservist in 1950, having completed a year of active duty at Fort Sill, Oklahoma, where I had been trained in the latest Fire Direction Control System and where I had worked as part of a school troop instruction group in the Artillery School. This was a change from the Fire Direction Control System used in

World War II and was being introduced to the Army as an improvement for Forward Observers to adjust fire on the enemy.

I gave no thought to being recalled. I was basking in my successes and looking ahead to a bright future with Florence. My hopes were high. I was on cloud nine, as most people would say. But the euphoria was not to last. It was shortly after the first of July when I received a disturbing letter from the government notifying me that I was on the critical list for recall. I was instructed to remain available and prepared to report for active duty on short notice because of my reserve status and my military MOS (Military Operational Specialty), which was FDC. The news struck me like a blow between the eyes. I was mentally unprepared for the shock, as I knew that recall would disrupt my plans for the future and put our forthcoming marriage on hold, perhaps indefinitely. Like so many other reservists, the war in Korea suddenly took on a entirely new meaning.

The die was cast at that point. There was nothing I could do but wait. I realized it was just a matter of time before I would be called up to support the war effort in Korea, in the continental United States, or elsewhere. It was not until I joined the 8th FA Battalion in December that I heard the facts from the surviving members of the 8th FA. I was to be one of the replacements for those who were lost in the disaster of August 22, 1950, when the FDC tent was hit by a mortar round.

After receiving notice that I might be recalled, Florence and I had an urgent discussion that culminated in a firm and irrevocable decision. We would be married before I left for active duty. Florence and I had met in high school. We were deeply in love. There was nothing that would break us apart, not even a war in a distant country we knew little about. We discussed our intentions with our parents. They understood we were serious. With their approval, we went ahead with our wedding plans.

I received my recall letter shortly after Labor Day in September and reported for my physical examination in the Federal Building on Lake Street in Minneapolis as requested. Two weeks later I was told that I had passed the physical and that my reporting date was scheduled to occur the first few days in October.

Florence and I didn't say too much about our plans to anyone until after we met with the minister of Florence's home church, St. Anthony Park Methodist, on the morning of September 21. That morning, as we entered the pastor's office, his smile, and the shift of his eyes, were indications that he already knew why we had asked for the meeting. After his handshake, he asked what he could do for us.

My answer was direct, without hesitation. I said we wanted to get married. His smile broadened. He asked if we had selected a wedding date. Again, I was direct. Tomorrow, I said bluntly.

My reply startled him somewhat. He sat down behind his desk, smoothed his fingers, one hand over the other, then tilted his head humorously while reminding me that tomorrow was a bit early, that certain arrangements had to be made, a marriage license for starters. He asked if I had applied for one.

I told him we had not. I didn't know the procedure. Getting married was new to me. Without pause, he reached for the phone, lifted the receiver, grinned again. He placed the call directly to the license bureau, asked a few questions, found out that the earliest we could pick up the marriage license was Tuesday, September 26. It didn't give us much time, eight days at the most, to put the whole thing together.

Immediately after the meeting we dashed to the license bureau. A clerk welcomed us, a middle-aged lady who seemed somewhat oblivious to the importance of her station. She was intensely nonchalant as we paid the fee and began filling out the application. When I was finished, she took it in hand, read the information we had supplied, then looked at me over the top of her glasses. Her eyes squinted as she conveyed the problem. I was not twenty-one.

Another roadblock, and I was driving very fast. In my brashly insistent manner, I told her we had to get married right away. I was leaving for the Army. We couldn't wait.

She replied calmly that we would need our parents' approval, their signature on the document. I was anxious, insistent. Florence gripped my arm. When? How? We didn't have time.

The clerk assumed a more composed attitude, as if she was about to notch her pencil with one more good deed. She told me the office closed at 4:30, but promised that if I took the application home and had my parents sign it, and returned it by 3:30, she'd process the signed copy and have the license ready for us on Tuesday morning, September 26.

I don't remember what I told her, but it was something in the way of a thank you. We had a chance, and left City Hall smiling. We had lunch with Mom and Dad at my home on Pascal Street and they signed it without hesitation. With this detail completed, we returned the application to City Hall before closing time. Our wedding date was set for Tuesday, September 26, 1950, on the chance that our license would be ready as promised.

Florence and I had the major job of organizing all the details for the wedding. Our mothers accepted the task of inviting people by telephone. They were both active in their respective churches and it was easy for them to call their usual list of friends and invite them to the wedding at 4:00 on the 26th. My Uncle and his new wife drove all the way from Chicago and made it in time. Other invited notables were the wife of the retired president of the University of Minnesota, representing the university where Florence's father was an assistant professor in agricultural engineering on the St. Paul Campus, and had been since 1903.

The wedding was simple. My very close friend since grade school was best man. Our close friend from the choir in Murray High School sang, and Florence's closest friend from grade school on was maid of honor. We were all close friends. The church was over half full, even with such short notice.

We left the reception that day about 6 PM and spent our first night together at the Leamington Hotel in Minneapolis. In the morning we left for a one-week honeymoon at a resort on White Fish Lake in northern Minnesota. It was not a modern retreat, but rather rustic in design. We survived a very cold week with the help of the owner who supplied us with wood stacked daily by our back door. We burned it as fast as he replaced the pile. We returned home on the 3rd of October and stayed at my parents' home on Pascal Street. My reporting date was to occur on the 9th or 10th of the month. The time between our return from the honeymoon and my leaving was extremely busy. As newlyweds, we were on a steady diet of parties and events, everyone wishing me "God speed and good luck." At that time the effect of World War II had worn off, but not all the way. Many of our friends remembered saying goodbye to men leaving then, and had gone through the joy of watching them return, or the sorrow of losing them. All who had lived through that era made a solid attempt to make our few remaining days together a happy time, for us and for our parents.

I left Minneapolis on the afternoon of October 10, in a military coach attached to the end of the North Coast Limited, with orders in my pocket. Our parents were at the station, Florence tight to my side. The men held steadfast and firm; the women wilted with the sorrow of separation, unable to believe I was leaving. With a lump in my throat, and a heart squeezed with turmoil, my hand was welded to hers, my eyes taking in her beautiful face, her eyes, the love that was there. Then the time came to go. I turned and walked away, looked back only once as my body went numb, gave them a wave, a smile of sorts as I melted into the groups of men standing beside the coaches. We were a rather large, well-disciplined group of men, from many parts of Minnesota and the five state area. I went inside, found a seat, felt as if I had been swallowed.

The group was divided into units of 10–15 men, with one man given the responsibility of being in charge of each group. I was placed in charge of one group, most of whom were stone-faced and confused, tight-jawed to demonstrate their bravery, resolute in purpose. It was easier for the officer to deal with leaders rather than the total number of men.

It was an uneasy ride. My eyes were riveted on the window for much of the time, looking at the passing countryside, which went by in a blur. My thoughts were home, where my heart was, because nothing lay ahead of me except confusion and uncertainty. As a young man still in civilian clothes, with a new wedding ring on my finger, I had plenty of time to think about what awaited me at my destination and what I had left behind.

My group had the best deal of the bunch because the captain who accompanied us was a friend of the sergeant in charge. He was responsible for getting us into a deluxe Pullman while the other GIs were billeted in a tourist car. The steward was a member of my home church, Elim Covenant in St. Paul. He had lost his son in World War II and had a warm spot for all soldiers. As a result, we ate in the diner, white tablecloths and napkins, silverware, while the others ate in a lunchroom set aside specifically for GIs. I ended up with a bunch of reservists in the same boat as I, some married, a couple with children. Separation was the hardest for them. We spent the time talking, found out that we were all disgusted, wanting to be elsewhere. There was little talk of the war. Most chose to ignore it. Instead, they told stories about how they came to be on the train, bits of life, laughing occasionally to break the spell of loneliness and the uneasiness of strangers. Some sat quietly, smoking, their thoughts suspended in wreaths of smoke, already missing the life they had left behind. I was the most recently married guy in the group, an honor I wore with pride.

We traveled that first day, going west through Fargo and Mandan, across the vast prairie, nothing for our eyes to see except visions of former times. Most of the time we just watched the ground fly by. The seats were good, coach seats, nothing fancy. But they would tilt down for comfort, and I dozed at times. When night came the porter converted the seats into Pullman berths. Narrow aisles. Bathrooms at the end of each coach. When the train was in a station all the bathrooms were closed because the discharge was directed to the railroad ties under the cars.

The second day took us through Missoula, into Logan, Utah, where the mountains reared up on both sides of the train, snow capped and massive on a radiant day, the sun warm through the window, making us seem even more insignificant than we already were. We stopped briefly in Spokane, then railed straight through by way of Seattle, where we changed coaches, then headed for Tacoma. There we boarded the post busses for Fort Lewis, the 94,000 acre Army reservation on the Nisqually River, home of the 2nd Infantry Division, named after Meriwether Lewis of the famed Lewis and Clark Expedition. In 1950 it was home to thousands of recalled reservists like myself, newly arrived, confused, frightened. None of us knew what to expect. The unknown was always hard to talk about.

The sky was cloudy that day. A gray mist hid the Cascades— weather appropriate to our moods. Rain was predicted for the remainder of the week. We were issued GI ponchos that were used by the Army as both a raincoat and a shelter-half when necessary. The edges had straps that could be put together to form a cover, with a hole for the head, a drawstring to tighten it. It was good cover for the Pacific Northwest. The ponchos were the total extent of our uniforms.

The first night in the barracks consisted of the usual small talk, handshakes, getting acquainted. Men were from everywhere—northerners, southerners, mountain boys, prairie dwellers. Lights went out at nine o'clock. We crawled in beneath our single brown woolen blanket, stared into the darkened room, listened to throats clearing, shuffling bodies, a calming down before the silence came on, then so still you could hear other men breathing. Sometime later, one of the men got up and went to the window and stood staring toward the East. I thought it was the small, tow-headed guy from Oklahoma but I couldn't be sure. Soon I heard him sob softly. I looked over at him. Moonlight lay white across his shoulders. No one told him to be quiet. Those who weren't sleeping just let him cry. I watched him for a while. My thoughts were also somewhere else, and in that unfamiliar space, filled with the muffled sounds of sleeping, I whispered into my pillow those words I would have spoken to Florence had I been back home. Sometime later I feel asleep.

2

FORT LEWIS, WASHINGTON

Friday started early, at 05:30. Dress fast. Move fast. Normal confusion. Uncertainty. Breakfast in the huge mess hall which served 1,400 men. Long lines beginning one hour before serving, lasting one hour later. Everyone better eat by then or it's shutdown time. Swift and furious. Take what you get. The food was good. Scrambled eggs and bacon.

Tests all that first day, 11 in all, the same as those I took when I was stationed at Fort Sill. They covered everything from general knowledge to radio specialist. I did quite well until I got to the last two. Radio and electricity weren't my forte. We were told that uniforms would be issued the following day. On Sunday we would get our shots. Filled out a report on dependents. Changed my insurance to $10,000 straight life. Hoped it would never be paid.

We still had no idea where we were going. The grapevine had it that we would be going overseas, to Korea, but no one was certain. Our training time was scheduled for 16 days, six being a field trip. The seven-day week was an indication that we were gearing up for something big, possibly combat. Loose talk. Rumors. No one knew what to believe. We heard that draftees would begin coming in the following week. We hoped we might end up as cadre, to teach the incoming conscripts a thing or two. But that was mere speculation.

On Saturday we went to the Classification Center to get our personal affairs in order. It is there they presented us with the worst possible scenario, death, and talked to us from that point of view. I learned my wife's pay allotment would be $127.50 per month, $67.50

10

from the government and $60 from my pay. Florence would begin receiving it in December.

After classification we went to clothing issue where they measured us, took our civvies, and started us down a long counter. There I received three shorts, three T-shirts, khaki shirts, socks, belt, brass, fatigues, helmet, helmet liner, gun belt and olive drabs.

First of all, personal equipment had to be marked with a permanent market with our identification number that was called a laundry number in a barracks situation. My number was H4587, my last initial and the last four digits of my serial number. They went on every piece of gear. The gun belt was an interesting addition. It was a heavy woven belt about two inches wide and a quarter inch thick, with eyelets every couple of inches. Every soldier had to carry a first aid pack that was hooked into one of the eyelets. Then came a canteen that was covered with canvas. When wet, the evaporation served to cool water inside the canteen. The covered canteen was the receptacle for the canteen cup, or coffee cup. The eyelets also allowed room to carry a clip of ammunition for your rifle or .45 pistol when you were issued one. I was not issued one until I became a sergeant.

Then came the combat boots. Unfortunately my size, 13D, was unavailable. After measuring me a second time they decided I should have a 13EE. Those were like a barge, way too wide, unacceptable. Next possibility, a 13E, which they also didn't have. After some deliberation they determined that I must have a 13½C, which was what they did have. The issuing quartermaster insisted that I put them on and give them a trial period. Knowing from past history that my feet would be in trouble with that size, I issued a firm objection, forgetting that I was no longer a civilian, but someone who must take orders without question. Outranked, and with the command firmly implanted in my transitional brain, I returned to the barracks wearing my new boots, standard issue, thick-soled, high top work shoes with a leather ankle strap about three inches wide above the shoe top, two more straps with buckles to hold it all in place. As fate would have it, someone had a football. To me, a football was like an ice-cold rootbeer on a hot day. Having played left tackle in both high school and at the University of Minnesota, I was drawn in, new boots and all. Before the game ended, my feet were a mess, a blister the size of a quarter on my heel, another on the side of my toe, split open, seeping. It was then I limped to the lieutenant, boots in hand. I found him in the barrack.

I grimaced along with a stiff salute, requested that he look at my feet. He was uninterested at first, until I lifted my foot. The damage was clearly evident. He scowled as his lips tightened. He asked how it happened.

I didn't mention the football game. I put the blame where it belonged. I told him Supply didn't have my size, that I was issued a smaller pair and told to wear them for a week. I had them on for only six hours when I entered his office.

His answer was abrupt. He asked me how I expected to train. I told him I wouldn't be able to train. One more day and I'd be in the infirmary. He rubbed his chin, took my shoes in hand and headed for the door, insisting that I follow him.

As was the lieutenant's nature, he used his rank to censure the quartermaster. In a rather blistering statement, he told him to order some properly sized boots from anywhere, and to get them to Fort Lewis in a hurry. He made it clear that his soldiers could not train without proper footwear. Until the boots arrived, I was permitted to wear my civilian shoes, an old pair of low-cut oxfords, already well worn and near replacement.

Shots on Sunday, tetanus, typhoid, the usual spread, arm as sore as a migraine but not as bad as when I had them at Fort Sill. Must be getting used to needles. We were marched from the medic station to another room where we watched training films, an "Introduction to the Army," another on the "Articles of War," a third on "VD," how to protect against it, and what happened if you didn't. The graphic pictures of genitals rotting away made one wonder if sex of any kind was worth the thrill.

Learned I was being transferred to a basic unit over on the North Fort. The training would be concentrated and would consist of rifle range, bivouac, crawling through obstacles, the mud course, beneath overhead fire with live ammunition. That would be followed by a 20-mile forced march. Thanks to the CO, I didn't have to participate in the march until I received my new combat boots, a blessing in disguise.

We moved from the reception center to North Fort Lewis on a rainy day, no clouds, sky the color of slate, a fine mist in our faces. Our training schedule was expected to be five days long, then a holiday, followed by another five on, one off, to be repeated a third time before being assigned to our final unit. The "chicken" outfit, as it was dubbed, would attempt to make real soldiers of us in the 15-day time frame. We were segregated according to the branch of service we had been in before. Our first stop was the clothing depot where we were issued another stack of clothes, our helmet, pack, blankets, sleeping bag, footlocker, other necessities. Then we were assigned to a tent where we would mark all items. I was in Barracks #6, assigned to Battery A, the 36th FA Battalion.

In the tent we talked openly about our situation. To the man, as United States citizens, we believed we did not belong in a Korean conflict, that was, to us, a civil war. We were soldiers, to be sure, but we joined the Army to defend our nation, not to fight someone else's battles. Some predicted this was merely a beginning, in which our country would be called upon to fight Communism wherever it raised its ugly head. Others disagreed. I turned in that night assuming that I would be assigned to a field artillery unit and that I would be going to Korea. Why else were we there? Deep inside, I knew I would eventually be thrust into combat, a role I had trained for but one I dreaded to fulfill.

The following morning we attended a lecture on the M-1 rifle, the infantry weapon, how to strip it, clean it, reassemble it, how to embrace it as your best and most reliable friend. Went to a dry firing range and practiced firing positions and sight pictures. Learned we would be going on bivouac. I would not go unless I got my boots, because my civilian shoes were giving out, soles wearing through, coming loose. Feet so damn sore I could hardly walk.

A poker game ensued that night on the bed, six guys in skivvies, lots of cursing, words I seldom heard back home, greenbacks changing hands as if it had little value. A kid from Texas walked away with most of the money, gloating, the others hangdog.

Another visit to the quartermaster proved futile. Still no boots. Went to the firing range where we sighted in the M-1 and Carbine on a 1,000-inch familiarization course. The soles separated from my shoes on the way back, became a flap, fastened only at the arch, loose under the balls of my foot. Water came through the insole, made mush of my stockings. I would not be going to the big firing range the next day because I had no combat boots to wear. My feet were rebelling, sore and bleeding.

That night we had a GI barracks party, cleaned the floors, scrubbed everything for inspection. We did well. Everyone pitched in willingly, not a rummy in the bunch.

Mail finally came, letters from home, those indescribably beautiful pages with familiar writing, words of love, encouragement. I could hear Florence's voice as I read. Her words lingered through the day and well into the night, were still there after the lights went out. How much better mail made me feel. I read them again the next day, while alone in the barracks. Everyone else had gone to the firing range.

My new shoes arrived on the 21st, but they were the high-top version, not combat boots, thin soled, the type mechanics wear. But they were all I had, good enough for light duty, not good enough for marching. I threw away my old ones that were then held together with tape. I received the shoes just before I talked with the first sergeant about my extra duty. I approached him with a thought in mind, something I had done when I was at Fort Sill. At the time, he seemed intent on dismissing me before I spoke, but I beat him to the punch. I told him I wanted kitchen work, that I wouldn't mind fitting into the outfit as a permanent fixture.

With a grin comprised of half surprise and half laughter, he asked me why I wanted to do KP. I told him I'd done it before, that I was experienced and capable. I enjoyed cooking. I was good at it. I gave him every conceivable reason why he should consider my request.

He turned his head doubtfully, as if to imply that reservists were experienced in everything except soldiering. But since I was willing to do what no one else wanted to do, he said he'd look into it.

He approached me the next morning with the news I had been waiting for, that I was to be 2nd cook. I was given my apron, along with a word of encouragement. He said if everything went well it could be a permanent station, that he was sending in a request for transfer to Brigade.

I made chicken noodle soup that day, heavy on the broth, helped chop vegetables for salad, washed pots. I'd do anything to remain stateside, closer to Florence. Besides, cooking was a preferred alternative to being shot at. I was beginning to think I had Fort Lewis licked, until the transfer came back marked, REFUSED. Furthermore, it stated, I would be required to take all the training except for the forced marches, until my feet healed up. I was given permission to ride in the truck wherever I went. But the refusal didn't stop me from pursuing the kitchen idea. I talked to another sergeant, a tall blonde Swede from Superior, Wisconsin. He said he would do whatever he could to keep me in the States, because we both knew that if a transfer didn't work for me, it was overseas for sure. Putting in for OCS was also out. I was ER (Enlisted Reserve). I couldn't get anything like Officers Candidate School unless I signed up for additional duty. The Army would not make any promises on OCS unless it was backed up with a five-year commitment.

When we went on bivouac the next day, I had a gut feeling that things would never really change. I was bound for Korea, just as sure as the geese were flying south.

We were up the next morning at 04:15, left the barracks at 06:00. I was in a 2½-ton standard truck, the type of vehicle used to transport both equipment and men. It was covered with a canvas top, had seats on each side. The truck was loaded with all the bedding the men couldn't carry. It made me feel like a slacker. I wasn't about to hike in footwear that was already creating problems for me.

We were on the rifle range at first light, firing for accuracy from standing, sitting, kneeling and prone positions, five rounds each time. Then it was on to the combat course in the rain, splashing through the muck, sliding through the mud and rocks, shooting from behind stumps, brush piles, open windows, logs, similar cover that we might encounter in a combat situation. It was good training. The targets were at different distances, and of different types, ranging from 25 yards to 525 yards. I fired a respectable score of 115 out of a possible 200, considering that we were not using our own weapons with which we had already become familiar enough to trust. After the firing we walked back two miles in the pouring rain. By that time my clothes were a mess. The road was dirt and gravel, half mud. I

15

refused a ride in the truck, as I didn't want to be looked on as a piker. I was dead tired when we pulled up, feet hot as hellfire, only to learn that we had a "Night Problem" facing us. I, nor anyone else, had not the faintest idea of what it was all about.

We slept outside in the rain in a summer sleeping bag, on ground as cold as winter snow. The summer bag was made of a heavy cloth-type material inside and a protective cover outside. It was adequate against dew, but not rain, and at Fort Lewis it rained all the time. When the cloth got wet, the bag was useless. Wind, much more than a whisper and chilled with heavy air, came in through every opening of the bag, made it damp inside, dirty and foul, the smell of sweat in my nostrils, goosebumps fretting along my arms. My teeth chattered twice. I curled up like an armadillo, into a ball of quaking flesh. Exhaustion finally took me away into a sleep interrupted a dozen times by noises. Korea wouldn't be any better, I thought. It would be winter when we arrived over there. I'd never be able to sleep outside in the winter. God, I prayed, don't let me freeze to death. Tried to sleep again. Knew I had to get up at 04:30 when it was dark and still cold in the moonglow. I hated the Army that night. The only warmth at all came with thoughts of Florence.

Returned to barracks the next day, listened to a lecture on first aid and sanitation, then prepared for bivouac again. Had time to call home. Talked to Florence. For a moment I forgot about the cold and the rain and the miserable conditions and melted into her voice. Remembered that the next day, the 26th, would be our one-month anniversary. Took the glow of that call with me for the entire day and night, until we were rousted out again at 03:20 the following day.

In the darkness before dawn, the boys left on foot. I was again in the truck. Three miles later we stopped at the combat village where, in mock situations, we practiced house-to-house fighting. But before combat drills started we had to scale three walls, eight, ten and twelve feet high. The first two were makeable, but with the slick-soled high-topped mechanic boots, I couldn't scale the twelve-footer, and gave the drill up as a bad cause. Then we had classes on various stages of the village and what to expect. Finally at 14:30 we were placed into squads of nine, given blanks for our M-1s and a grenade for each man. The object was to go from house to house and not get caught by any booby trap that had been planted indiscriminately. In the process we were to shoot at targets that would pop up when least expected, just like an enemy.

We broke up at 15:30. The sick, lame and lazy rode back in the trucks. Everybody's feet were in bad shape.

That night we had a bad accident in the battery. On the way back, after dark, a car slammed into the rear of the column. Twelve men were injured, eight seriously. The first sergeant was out with both his legs broken. As for the guys in our barracks, they escaped untouched.

By Friday, October 29, things were beginning to slow down. After the infiltration course, where we crawled on our stomachs under live machine gun fire three feet above our heads, we were given time to care for our equipment and to receive more shots, a sure sign that we were going overseas. Late that same afternoon six of us went to the service club and had hamburgers in a basket, pie, and coffee, a feast fit for a king, a great improvement over K-rations.

Rained again on Saturday, blustery winds, everything wet and cold. Didn't do much. Watched poor "Mac" trying to find his way over unfamiliar terrain by map. Mac is a name connected with all training films, a guy who gets himself into hopeless situations. Spent all afternoon in field artillery classes. Got more shots. Will they ever end?

I still did not have my regulation combat boots. I decided to go to the first sergeant and find out what was delaying them. He was still trying to keep me stateside, seemed determined to do so, was trying to get my boots as soon as he could. I was sure he would give me a break.

We heard many rumors about the position of the reserves. One fellow received a paper stating that civilian jobs and occupations would hold some weight when it came to assignment, but we really didn't believe that. We also heard that they had stopped calling up the reserves, were going to rely on the draft instead. Great. Made me feel like a guinea pig.

On the last Sunday in October I went to church on the post, then went to the mess hall only to find that they were not serving.

At the post club I had a steak dinner. At 14:00 I reported as directed and spent the afternoon in the rain, in the field, for a senseless class on field artillery, returned at 16:00 and out again at 18:00 for a night problem, in the infernal rain again. Found out that our training had been moved back one day, that we would not know our assignments until the 3rd. We were not told much. Rumors prevailed. A point system was explained that would determine our assignment. A low number meant Korea. A high number could mean a discharge.

The point system allowed one point for every three months of active service, one point for every month of overseas active service, one point for every year over 20 years of active service, two points for every medal of commendation, one point for every year in the reserve, and finally eight points for every dependent. I had a booming 14 points compared to a high of 94. The lowest point in our battery was four. The average was a 26. The system would allow them to discharge from the top down, and ship over from the bottom up. I was destined to go to war.

That afternoon I shouldered my way into a poker game, thirty pennies between four of us. At least we were out of the rain. The sun had shown only once in the past week and then for only a few minutes. I wondered where all the rain came from. It was cold and raw, with winter on the way. Went to a movie that night: *Emergency Wedding*. It passed the time.

My new high-top shoes were already beginning to fall apart when we went to the infiltration course, one hundred yards of barbed wire entanglements, explosives set to go off as we crawled through the mud. Our boys were shooting fairly high that day but it still made me hug good old mother earth as if I wanted to wear it. We started out in a pit, on our own, rifle slung over one arm, as pancake flat as we could get, stomachs scraping the ground. When I came to the mined area, a charge went off right in my ear, shook me like an earthquake, left a ringing in my head, like a thousand jangling telephones. Crawled again, dust in my eyes, came to the wire entanglement, wormed my way through on my back, under the snaking barbed wire, past more mines. A guy from Detroit came through behind me, grunting with every breath. He had no business being in the army. He was a reservist who no doubt passed his physical because he was warm, and had a heartbeat. His weight should have been under 200 pounds, but he was nothing more than flabby fat. When he was about ten yards behind me he started yelling, screaming and scared, his voice a high falsetto: "Help me! For Christ sake, help me!" He was stuck in the barbed wire, wrapped up like a chicken. The more he wiggled, the tighter he got. Every time the live ammunition screamed overhead, he yelled his lungs out. They had to shut down the total system and call in help to get him extricated from the wire. Eventually they carried him out, his eyes hollow and blank. Then they resumed the flights. That was the last we ever saw of him. Korea seemed closer all the time. Some said the drills were only a tenth of what combat was actually like, where fear would be great enough to last forever.

We went through the same thing that night, with tracers overhead, white hot streaks blazing through the blackness, howling sound, like a devil's voice. Lots of agonizing physical work. Agony. Cold sweat in my armpits. Mud caked in my ears, its acid taste in my mouth. Water in my pants. It was the longest 100 yards I ever crossed. Made a football field look like an inch. I slept like a stone that night. Never heard a whimper.

By the time the 2nd of November rolled around our training was over and then the wait began. They called for cooks, so I fell out of line and became 2nd cook in Mess #1 on the first shift. It would be the end of the month before we knew our destination. I thought it possible that I could remain in Mess #1 for my total service period. But that was only dreaming.

I went to work at noon. We were at full strength with a good crew. We cooked a meal. All went well until the first sergeant announced that we could expect 80 more men, but we didn't have enough food for them. I worked very late, went to bed at midnight, was the only one left to pull the morning shift. We had fried eggs, a major problem when we had only one grill and a wood stove. The mess hall was a cold place. The grate in the potbelly stove broke. We could see our breath in the air. Our barracks were no better. The grates there were also broken. The old stoves couldn't stand being placed into operation after standing idle for so many years. We didn't have any hot water either. Then orders came to shut the mess hall down. It was my responsibility to see that it was completely washed. Learned that 120 new men were coming in, with lots of cooks. My chance to remain on as a cook was thrown out with the wastewater. My mechanics boots rotted out as I was finishing my work.

I finally realized that I was going overseas. All men with points from 5 to 20 were destined for Korea. It was at that point that my new boots came along, still not the regulation combat boots but good enough to get me through the remainder of the training. I wrote home telling everyone not to send food or cookies until I received a more stable address.

Rained again, a fairly bad storm but no flooding. I moved to the cooks' barracks, had some time on my hands, wrote letters, stocked up on stamps and stationary for the long haul. Took an overnight pass and spent the night at the Moore Hotel in Seattle, Room 403. The first order of business was to call Florence.

It was a godsend to find a private telephone, away from the post, where you had to stand in line at a pay phone and get interrupted by loud and long "catcalls" if your conversation extended beyond three minutes. In the hotel I talked at my leisure, and listened to her wonderful voice in return. Without need to mask the obvious, I told her we were headed for Korea. I explained that I'd be in the artillery, about three miles behind the front lines, in a safe zone. I hoped she didn't know that there was no such thing as a safe zone. I added that my morale was high and joked that the war would be over quickly. The enemy would surrender when they learned I was coming.

She laughed, told me I was an eternal optimist, said that her marriage to me was the best day of her life. She wanted to go back to White Fish when I came home. I agreed. I told her I'd have a new address before I left. I'd call her one more time.

We talked on and on, recalled many things, planned others for the day I returned. She told me about our close friends, how our folks were doing, said she'd send some cookies, the snickerdoodles I loved. She'd keep the letters coming. Everything sounded normal back home. Hanging up was sorrowful. I laid on the bed and closed my eyes, pushed back the invading tears and allowed her words to seep into my soul.

On Sunday I went to services at the Swedish Covenant Church

in Seattle, was surprised to find two old friends from St. Paul's Elim Church. This couple was excited to see me. After the church service we had a good visit. They invited me on a ride through Seattle, to the seaport, then out to dinner at a fine restaurant. I had a T-bone steak. We talked for an hour about St. Paul. They said they had received an announcement of our wedding but nothing about my being in the Army. After finishing our meal we went to Andy's folks' home in Tacoma where I spent the evening. While I was there I showed them pictures of our wedding. I had a great time talking to civilians. It took away the strain of Army life, if only for a while.

They returned me to the Fort late that night. When I got to my barracks, I found out that I had to move downstairs.

I received my final orders on November 6, to report to F.E.C.A. (Far East Command Area) for a November shipping date. My destination was Fort Lawton, the port of embarkation. From there it was shipboard. I still didn't have my combat boots. I was wearing those usually issued to mechanics. I packed, then waited for the Greyhound bus that would take me and the others to Fort Lawton.

The bus didn't arrive. As a unit we marched to the assembly area in the North Fort, where we spent the night in a barracks. We were arranged by numbers on our shipping orders. It was a place where they collected men for disposition. We were 400 in all, 200 from our outfit, another 200 from the 11th AA battalion.

We loaded on Greyhound busses at 09:00 and rode to Pier 91, on Puget Sound, a Navy base used for preliminary processing. We ate and had a shakedown inspection for all extra clothing and civilian clothes. The inspection brought us down to 65 pounds of baggage for air shipment to Japan via the flying boxcar, going by way of Alaska, the Aleutians, a total of 72 hours flying time. They didn't waste any time with us.

We were billeted in a Navy barracks, a two story cement structure with all the comforts, tables, benches, showers, double bunks, a definite improvement over the standard Army bed. The Navy boys sure knew how to live and eat. We hadn't eaten this good since I left our kitchen back home. The food they put out for us was a hundred percent better than the portions at Fort Lewis. I met some friends that had been in the 6th Armored in Fort Sill, Bruce from Chicago and Henry from St. Cloud. We reviewed some past history, over-came the strangeness of our new surroundings.

The following day they reviewed my records, inspected them for error in insurance and allotment. They changed my MOS, not in number, but in wording. They had me classified as FDC and Liaison. Liaison was not good. It meant that I would be a forward observer. I told them I was a straight FDC, what I was trained for, and urged that I be reassigned accordingly. At any rate, I was to belong to an artillery unit, much better than being assigned to infantry. After record check I received a $105 pay. I sent Florence $95 and kept the rest for myself. Learned that we would leave Pier #51 for Fort Lawton, there to await our final orders.

We moved to Fort Lawton on Friday, November 10, into a hole they called a camp. The barracks were one story, sided with tarpaper, two wood stoves for 60 men, one stove at each end of the building. Every night someone was assigned to tend the fires. If they went out there would be no hot water for the showers. Not a good billet. We immediately went into another clothing check, were issued a jacket that goes under our field jacket, a wool lined affair with tight wrists, waist and neck. It was called a pile coat and was the first sensible piece of warm clothing I had been issued. I found myself in a big operation. With every move we made, they called a roster of 600 names. It took them three hours to call the roll in order to get us into the barracks. I was number 1,177, assigned to bunk 58. I was in the bottom group in the barracks. I ate in a consolidated mess hall located about a mile from my bunk.

After lunch we stopped by the PX to send a registered check to Florence. Got word that we may not fly to Japan. Our detachment was scheduled to leave on the 14th and rumor had it that a big liner would take us on. Good news in a way. I expected it would take a month to sail from here to Japan. I hoped it would be a short war. Perhaps it would be over by the time we arrived. Teamed up with one of the Minnesota boys, George from Minneapolis. Had some laughs. Talked about fishing, skiing, hockey and football. Passed the time.

Wrote a letter home that night, next to the wood stove that had a light over it. It was the first time in a month that I had the opportunity to write at a table. It was relaxing. Everyone else was sleeping. Very quiet in the barrack. Someone snored down the line. I gave Florence my new APO address.

I called Florence again on Sunday, had a wonderful conversation, held on to the sound of her voice until a couple of the men dragged me away to the PX. I weighed myself on the PX scale, came in at 230 pounds, fully clothed. Not too bad, considering the training I had been through. I expected I would lose much more weight once I was on field rations. George and I tried to go to town, to church, but the MPs stopped us and sent us back to our barracks. We went to the post chapel, like we should have done in the first place, prayed there, found peace in God's presence.

Late that day, when the boys finished KP, they received passes until 02:00. The fellow that slept below me didn't want to use his pass, so I took advantage of it with two other men. We went into town, walked past the closed shops, looked into store windows, breathed the smell of the streets still damp from the rain, smells different than the post, reminiscent of home. We found a small cafe and had Crab-Louis with all the trimmings. It was fun acting like civilians again, if only for a short time. Our last hurrah. Time was running out for us.

The next morning I rolled out later than the others, missed breakfast. By the time I was washed and dressed at 09:00 they had another shakedown inspection, ordering us to lay out everything we had. I never did fully comply. With 600 men involved it was impossible to check everyone thoroughly.

We were then ordered to stencil our duffels for shipping to the 374th Provisional Company that was to sail aboard the troop ship *General Freeman*, which held 5,200 men. It was to be part of an eight-ship convoy. Its destination was Japan.

That night we went to a movie which was interrupted by an announcement that all "B" detachment must return to their barracks because they were on orders. I began to sweat the fact that we might be leaving that night, that I wouldn't have an opportunity to call Florence. Fortunately it was just a precaution to prevent us from leaving the area. I placed my last telephone call that night.

We were up at 03:00 the following morning. Turned in our

blankets and rifle, then stuffed all the items we had not packed into our duffel, into a cargo pack, which we carried as a handbag. Including time to eat breakfast, the entire makeready took until 04:30. Then we stood by and waited, looked at one another, questioned what was going on. Some smoked. Others idled. A few leaned against the building as if to sleep on their feet. We started to leave at 06:30, first one group, then another. After a couple of roll calls, they took the first of our group at 09:00. The last half, that included me, waited until 10:30 to leave. We were loaded into many 6 × 6 trucks, 16 men to a truck, and in an escorted convoy of 20 trucks were taken through Seattle to Pier #39 where the newly painted troop ship, *General Freeman*, awaited us.

I was quartered on "E" deck, three levels below the main deck, but still above the waterline. I had the fourth bunk up from the deck. No one used the top one. Some of the men crammed their equipment up there to get it out of the way. None of us had much room considering that we had to squeeze our belongings into the two feet of space—our rifle, gas mask, helmet, clothing, duffel, everything. The best way to get in was to crawl in from the end. Also within that two feet we had to sleep, sit, get dressed, and do whatever else needed to be done. What little space remained in the passageway was sometimes crammed with men, all inside a compartment that held about 150 troops and gear. It was usually shoulder-to-shoulder, butt-to-butt, elbow-to-elbow. Troop ships were designed to carry men and that is all. The bunks were fairly good with a mattress, sheets, two blankets. I expected I would be warm enough. Bunks were to be made up at all times and inspected twice daily.

We were shipboard, but still in Puget Sound. Smooth water. I expected I would be sick once we hit the open sea. Our section 2-E was located directly under the bow. I knew that once we left the Sound, I'd be in for a rough ride.

We left port at 15:30 with little fanfare, only a small band to see us off, several groups on the pier waving, huddled wives and families of the sailors, handkerchiefs at their eyes. The Navy boys handed us rolls of confetti for us to throw. It hung like colored snow harbor mist, then scattered in the wind. Going overseas was hardly an event to celebrate. Most everyone was quiet.

The haze followed the ship out of the harbor. Soon the music faded away. The pier and the people disappeared in the distance, giving way to the dark shape of land. We no more than entered the Sound when we had our first fire drill. Everyone had to try on a life jacket and stand by our assigned station. Mine was in lifeboat #4.

They attempted to organize us, but we were in disarray. No one knew what to do. We were informed that we'd catch KP one day on and two days off. All other details would be forthcoming. Rumor had it that we would not be in a convoy, that we'd be cruising alone. If that were true, it would be a 12-day crossing.

The sky was darkening when we cleared the Strait, steamed past Vancouver Island. We stood at the rails, jammed shoulder to shoulder, watched the United States slip into obscurity, saw daylight diminish behind the darkening peaks as a rim of lights freckled the shoreline, the last of the city sparkling like a faded gemstone that had lost its luster.

The catch in my throat was comprised of loneliness, sorrow, and perhaps a bit of fear, something I was sure the others felt as well. Home and loved ones left behind. A sense of loss. The futility of our venture strong in our minds, war our only outlook.

Nothing ahead of us but water. An ocean to cross.

3

THE CROSSING

I dreamt of Florence that first night aboard the *General Free-man*, of her coming into the bedroom, her hair brown as chocolate across her shoulders, her nightclothes a radiant silk, shifting as she walked, shimmering in the pale light of the single lamp beside the bed. She crossed the room that seemed a mile long, and came to me and leaned to kiss my lips and in that moment I saw her eyes, like cinnamon crystal, and heard her voice say, "Darling, come home."

Then I stirred and opened my eyes and saw the bottom of the bunk above me, as though it were a coffin lid and I drew a breath so loud I could not believe it was me who made the noise. I felt the ship underway, the shift of its massive weight churning everything inside me as though it were a liquid mass. Looked through the compartment at the silent, sleeping forms, heard a painful moan from a distance. Several men were on their feet going off in the direction of the head. Again the ship's motion, its sway a slow rocking, the sound of its engines reverberating through the bulkheads, trembling through the steel with shock enough to quiver my cheeks. I wanted the dream back, so strongly that my hands fisted. My breath came out like a growl. So close to home, yet so far away. It angered me to think they'd taken away my freedom, my wife, all the things that mattered to me, to fight a war I was against fighting.

The ship lurched again, a violent pitch that sent my stomach charging into my throat. Gagging, I crawled out of the bunk, into a passageway littered with duffels and rifles and everything else that would impede anyone's passage. I rocked against the bunks as the ship leaned, tried to keep my balance, used the bunks to steady my progress, and finally made it to the head. Four other men were there, heaving. The smell of vomit sickened me, brought my gorge into my throat. I made it to the trough, knelt down, opened my mouth, felt everything expel like a hot stew, coughed, wiped away the spittle.

I knelt for a while, gathering my strength, then stood. At that point the ship seemed to settle down. My legs trembled. My head was filled with cotton, my eyesight jaded. I started back toward my bunk, pausing occasionally to steady my legs. I crawled in, collapsed, burrowed under the blanket and tried to ignore the constant rising and falling of the great beast that had swallowed me.

I stayed in my bunk until eight the next morning, was aroused by voices, shifting men, cursing, the accumulated bedlam of the confused and disoriented. I found my clothes rolled up to one side, pulled them on, crawled out, caught the blank stares of other men who were no better off than I, sick-eyed, uneasy, uncertain of what to do.

I found the ladder/stairs to the main deck, went out into the cold morning air. The sky was steel gray, the sun a mere blur behind the overcast. A stiff north wind slanted down from starboard, colder than I expected, across a blue-black sea feathered with whitecaps, water stretching into infinity. I went to the rail, watched the horizon lift and fall, leaned out to cough up what was left in my stomach, watched the vomit whip against the side of the ship. Another guy nearby shook his head, stumbled back against a bulkhead, slid down and buried his face between his arms. We had been told to get at least two hours of fresh air every day, topside, and now I knew why. Better than the foul air below, better than the stifling quarters. I breathed deeply despite the cold, felt the fresh air gorge my lungs. The wind was numbing, winter cold from the Aleutians. I stayed topside for one hour, then went below, sat for a while crouched on the bottom of the ladder until an officer touched my shoulder. I looked up, saw sympathy in his eyes. He helped me back to my compartment, told me that if I stayed horizontal I was less apt to be sick. I took his advice.

The second day I stayed in bed, except to make occasional trips to the head, and to the evening meal, which was less than satisfying. Thursday was worse. I did not eat all day. Sick again.

Then my turn came for KP. It was my release from the torture of seasickness. From that day on I was fine, despite the continuous motion of the ship. I learned we were on the Great Circle Route, which would take us south of the Aleutian Islands. But that soon changed. Before the day was over, rumor had it that we were headed toward Midway Island, and that some of the married men would actually be stationed there. By that time I was experienced enough to realize that rumor was more prevalent than truth. I shrugged it off as mere scuttlebutt.

Third day at sea. Being a corporal, I was placed in charge of our section for KP. I had seven men under me. Their responsibility was to wash pots and pans and carry garbage out to the stern in 30-gallon containers and dump it off into our wake. All I did was sit and watch, and make sure the detail did as they were instructed. Good duty. The boys worked splendidly without my direction. I went out with them a few times, watched our wake stretch all the way to the horizon, was pleased to note that our direction was southward, away from the Arctic Circle. The sun came out, made the water bluer than it had been but still not warm enough to stay on deck for any length of time.

That night we were told our route had been altered. Our course would take us north of the Hawaiian Islands and Midway, a longer route but much easier on the ship and on our stomachs. We were told the vessel was in need of a major overhaul because of a crack in her hull. Rumor had it that she was shipping a lot of water. Scuttlebutt again. It made the men feel uneasy. Some among us couldn't swim.

Sunday was rough. I had no urge to go on deck as it was still cool outside, the sky gray again. I stayed in my bunk, slept the day away, only traveled to the head and to the mess hall for meals. Thought a lot about home, the things Florence and I did in high school, our dates, our laughs, our love. Those past days sustained me through an unreal adventure that may have otherwise broken my spirit. It came to me several times that I was going to war. I didn't want to think about it, but it was always there, on the edge of my thoughts. Back home I couldn't even buy a beer because I was underage. Now I was being thrust into a conflict that could very well take my life. Unfair, I thought. Someone had said once that soldiers were cannon fodder. I shuddered to think that my life was suddenly meaningless, that I was expendable to powers greater than my own. It made for restless sleep.

On Monday the weather took a turn for the better. It was still chilly and uncomfortable topside. We had to wear our pile jackets when we went on deck. Had another fire drill. The bell rang. Everyone went to their compartment and put on their life jackets, then waited for the "Abandon Ship" signal. Three blasts, a short pause, three more blasts. We made tracks up the ladders to our boat station, 7A. The optimum time to reach our station was four minutes. Despite our haste, we were always unable to meet it. We knew there would be another drill soon. There was always another one.

Tuesday was our day for KP and also for compartment inspection. We hoped to duck the inspection but could not. They checked us on the main deck for clean clothes, shave, haircuts and general appearance. It was a way to kill a day. That evening, after KP, I took a shower and found that the machinery used to convert salt water to fresh water was out of service. I had to be content with a salt-water shower. That was practically like not taking a shower at all. At least the soap smelled good. I learned to appreciate fresh water.

Later my compartment buddy and I went to the fantail and tied our fatigues on a throw line, washed them by dragging them in the ocean. We couldn't leave the clothes in the salt water for more than four minutes. Any longer than that and they would be reduced to shreds. The screws churned the water into a white froth, mixed it right into the fatigues. We were traveling about 20 miles per hour, fast enough to make 325 to 425 nautical miles in a 24-hour period. They posted the distance traveled every day in the "dope" sheet, otherwise known as the "Plan of the Day." We relied on the sun for direction.

By Wednesday the weather had changed. Jackets were no longer in style. T-shirts were in full bloom. A brilliant sun. Rolling waters not choppy enough for whitecaps. The only sound on deck came from the blowers and the throb of the engines and the sound of the sea washing past our hull. I had not been issued a T-shirt because of my size. I had a fatigue shirt instead. It was adequate enough if I didn't tuck it in.

We had four showings of movies on board each day. I saw *Three Came Home*, a story about the war in New Guinea. Also, *Francis the*

Talking Mule. We laughed aloud at that one, especially when the mule talked a 2nd lieutenant into the ground. Another was *Broken Arrow*, an Indian picture about the Apache chief Cochise. The theater was in one of the compartments that measured about 20 feet long and 15 feet wide. Fully loaded it held about 200 men, all seated. Occasionally the movies were held on the fantail—more room, more men. The sea was calmer but it was still odd to watch a movie with the ship swaying as it did, men sitting shoulder to shoulder, knee to back, crowded together on a hard steel deck.

Thursday, November 23, brought Thanksgiving to the ship. I attended services on the fantail. Was glad that we had a religious service to go along with the holiday, although it was inadequate compared to the celebrations back home. We did have turkey, two pieces, with all the trimmings—potatoes, cranberry sauce, cheese and rolls— followed by pumpkin pie with ice cream. The mess hall was decorated with streamers. There was candy on the aluminum tables. As we left they gave us each an apple and an orange. I ate them both at the rail, tossed the apple core into the sea, imagined what it was like back home. Memories enough to last the day.

On Thursday we crossed the International Date Line. I went to bed Thursday night and woke up on Saturday morning. Lost an entire day. They had a date line ceremony on the main deck. The officers walked around with their pants rolled up to their knees, like we were supposed to do, lipstick smeared on their faces. I guess crossing the line is really a Navy thing. We soldier boys were quite unimpressed with the ceremony. But it was fun. We sang a few songs, had some laughs. All in all, the change was appreciated. By this time the routine had become sheer boredom.

KP again—same men, same detail. It was so hot in the galley that I helped carry garbage to the fantail, just to get some fresh air. Long, deep swells on the sea.

It was then we learned about the dumbwaiter. The officers' food was prepared in the kitchen next to ours. All the food had to go up a dumbwaiter to the wardroom. On one particular day we were loading apple pies into the dumbwaiter when one of my men turned to me and asked why the officers got all the good stuff, while we got only pudding.

I told him it was a matter of rank. Besides, I said, we were just dogfaces. He looked at the pies, said he didn't think they'd miss a couple. We hadn't had pie since we left the States. I looked around at several of the guys who were salivating at the sight of the pies. Two of them nodded. All I had to do was motion. The response was instantaneous.

So we took the pies, eight in all. And we never heard a word. That made it easy for us to pilfer the dumbwaiter whenever something good caught our eye. We were doing okay until the officers missed a five-gallon bucket of ice cream. It took a lieutenant JG about fifteen minutes to slide down the ladder and push his way into the kitchen. He was livid. He wanted to know where their ice cream was and who was in charge.

The men pointed at me. By this time the ice cream was gone, well on the way through the men's digestive systems. I shrugged my shoulders, said I knew nothing about missing ice cream. No evidence, no case. The officer looked at each man in turn; demanded an explanation. He was met with more shrugs. Not a single man cracked a smile.

The officer turned on me with a stiff finger at my nose. With all the weight of his authority behind him he told me that one more theft on the dumbwaiter would earn me a trip to my commanding officer. Men, he said, had been court-martialed for less.

He was Navy. I was Army. I figured it was about time I stood my ground. Defiantly, I asked him if that meant I'd get to go home, instead of going to war.

The lieutenant gave me a DI sneer. His eyes narrowed as he scanned his audience. With the last of his bravado, he issued a warning: One more trick like this and we'd all go to the brig. He swung around and stormed out of the kitchen, having made his point. It was the last time we pilfered anything from the dumbwaiter.

Immediately following that incident, when my temperament was at an explosive pitch, one of the men approached me carrying a 68-pound tub of butter. He hefted it in his arms and asked what he was supposed to do with it. I told him I didn't know; that for all I knew they kept it in the oven.

It wasn't an order or a command, just a dumb statement. But

31

like every soldier, he did as he was told and shoved the butter into the oven. What followed just about got me a court-martial. The butter melted. It was all over the oven, on the deck, everywhere, all 68 pounds of it. Cleaning it up was a total mess. Many trips to the fantail. But despite our theft of the dumbwaiter and melting a tub of butter, we were a good crew. We were rated on cleanliness and work habits on a daily basis and our crew always scored high. We knew we had a chance to get the steak dinner when the final ratings were scored. A steak dinner was enough to make us all toe the mark.

One of the guys who slept close to me had a fit one day. He yelled, screamed, threw everything he could get his hands on, threatened others with bodily harm, swore a silver streak. He went berserk, like a madman, had to be subdued by several others. They dragged him away to sickbay, probably tied him down. I doubt if he ever made it to Korea.

Besides KP, all we did was eat, sleep, walk the crowded decks, look at the endless expanse of water. On occasion we saw another ship, a freighter, another trooper. We passed a school of porpoises and watched the flying fish skim the surface of the waves off our bow.

The interior of the ship was always hot. We were in warmer waters then. Men lounged everywhere, against the bulkheads, on the decks, playing cards, writing, sleeping, throwing a bundled-up sock for a ball, exercising. Most of the guys stayed to themselves. I sat in my bunk when it was cool enough, leaned against my pack, used an empty candy box for my desk, wrote to Florence. My ties with home were becoming more and more important to me.

It was easy for me to find buddies to chum with. They came from St. Paul, Minnesota, Des Moines, Iowa, Detroit, Michigan, and northern Minnesota. Was fortunate enough to bump into a neighbor, from St. Paul. Found out that he left for the service the day after I was married. He lived on Arona, two doors down from my best man. He was billeted back near the stern.

Rough water again, the sky choked with clouds. There were long deep swells capped with white foam, wind strong enough to keep us below decks, and rain sweeping along the decks. Some said we were on the fringe of a typhoon. It was rough enough to make the rumor believable. Late in the day it calmed down, and by sunset the sky was blue again, the sunset radiant, gold and purple among the retreating clouds.

My bunky and I had the idea to sleep on deck that night, even though we knew the Navy boys would chase us below and they did, at 22:00 hours. Instead of going below, we found a narrow spot under an outside ladder, spread out a blanket, and tried to sleep. We lasted only a half hour. The deck was too cold and hard for either of us. We spent a few minutes at the rail, looking into the darkness, at the mass of stars above. We'd never seen so many stars.

His eyes drifted to the white water skimming past the ship. He asked me if I thought we'd be coming home. There was desperation in his voice.

I told him the only thing I could, the very thing I pinned my hopes on, that the war would be over soon because of all the men and materials that were pouring into South Korea. I added that the Koreans would be glad we came.

He looked at me then, his eyes adrift in doubt. He laughed prophetically, said that someday the Koreans would forget what we did for them. He was firm in his belief that two generations after the war was over they'd snub their noses at us. I couldn't disagree.

We went to our sacks, set our watches back another hour, 17 hours' difference from the clocks back home. It would end up 16 hours' difference before we docked.

Scrambled eggs and fried potatoes for breakfast. If it wasn't for an occasional apple and orange, it would become monotonous.

On deck the sun was warm, the air cool, funnel fumes hanging low. Strolled topside for a few hours. Later on, we headed in a northerly direction again. Pile jackets were being worn. By late afternoon we were taking water over the bow, heavy seas, stiff wind. Never realized how quickly the sea could change.

Below, two of the men had borrowed guitars from the ship's library. We all crowded into our compartment as they sang songs, old favorites we could sing along with. We had over 100 guys in one spot. A little fleshy fellow took over MC duties. We had a good time despite the rolling of the ship.

KP again the following day. During breakfast the lieutenant

came around and told us the outcome of the contests. We were 15 points in front of the second unit with a score of 96 percent. We realized we had to do a terrific job to win. All the men turned to that day and did an outstanding job cleaning and polishing. When it was over, we attained a top score of 98 percent dining room, and 90 percent galley. We had won the contest.

We pulled the noon meal with all the vim and vigor of the first day and had the afternoon off until 15:00. We all reported back on time. The steak dinner was served before the evening meal. It was a T-bone with all the trimmings. The NCOs served the meal. The lieutenant checked to make sure that no outsiders had invaded our ranks. We had steak, mushroom sauce, French fries, orange juice, hot rolls, ice cream, cookies and a cake decorated in big letters that read, "Well done KPs." We ate like kings, and we all appreciated the recognition. That night we finished our last KP for the trip.

The next day, our final day at sea, was routine. I spent time sitting in the day room, waiting for night to arrive, and I wrote letters. Skimmed through a book from the library, couldn't concentrate. The weather on deck was cool, with the usual rainsquall. We sat around and talked over the war news, which was not good. The boys were beginning to realize that we would be on the Korean front, in midwinter. Not a thing we could do about it. Follow orders. Take things as they come. Hope that an angel would be on your shoulder. The how and why of the war was beyond anyone's comprehension. We had all grown up during the Second World War, had seen newsreels of Africa, Sicily, Italy, France, Guadalcanal, Tarawa, Iwo Jima, all the battles, all the blood. We were still unprepared for what was to come. We had only visions of what it was like. We had not yet acquired fear.

After dinner I went to a song service, and had a talk with the chaplain. I realized I had missed something by not talking to him before. The chaplain was a young fellow from Flint, Michigan, a Methodist. He had a couple of years in the service and was studying chiropractic science. He was an interesting man. We had a great talk, discussed the creation theory before he preached the sermon. He really knew his stuff. He put the truth across.

On deck that night, we were within sight of the beacons from

Tokyo. Many men crowded at the rail, looking toward land, our first stop on the way to war. Most were saddened, including myself, realizing we were so close to battle and so far away from those we loved.

We learned we would dock at 09:00 the following morning. At about 13:00 hours we would go to the 4th Repo. Depot. From there it was anyone's guess.

Our mail would be fouled up for a while. We hoped some would be waiting for us.

4

JAPAN

We entered Yokohama Bay late at night. I was awakened by the anchor chain chattering at the bow, heard mumbling in the compartment, went back to sleep until reveille, a fitful sleep with much tossing and turning. We were up at 05:00 for breakfast. The ship got underway again about 06:30, on its way to the pier.

Went on deck, watched as the ship crept toward its dock, through hordes of small fishing craft that appeared to be centuries old, with dirty sails, rusted metal, smoke puffing from their pipes, their engines chugging with a grieving exhaustion. They had no business floating. No one kept them away. They ringed our ship like floating locusts, tagged us all the way to the docks. The people on board looked no better than the boats. They were ragged, unkempt, blended in with the age and decay as if they had been created from the same materials. It was hard for me to believe that just five years earlier they had been our enemy. The only indication that they still had a Navy came with the passing of a single-stack Japanese destroyer that appeared to be almost as old as the fishing boats, rust being its only decoration.

Ashore we saw nothing but grim mountains, a sprawling city, dismal in the early morning hours, buildings gray and brown, blending with the landscape. No color apparent. Black cranes rising from the shipyards. As we neared the pier, young children, perhaps 10–15 years old, swam out in the oil-slicked water to beg from the men at the rail. How they could swim in the cold, dirty water was beyond me. I guessed it was a matter of survival. At any rate, it left a lasting impression on me. The smell of the Orient was heavy in the air, a strange new scent to which I would soon become accustomed.

We pulled into the wharf, a long concrete slab built on pilings, a huge warehouse beside it. Kids at dockside peered up in gray clothing, their hands outstretched for a tossed coin or a cigarette. They had learned several words of English very well. Their calls came like the chattering of monkeys. "Candy. Smoke. Coins." They remained there until our ship was tied up. When the gangways went out, they were shooed away, some having been successful in their foray.

We ate lunch on board, then gathered our gear and waited to debark for Camp Drake, where we would be quartered until we were ordered to ship out for Korea. We left the ship in single file, down the clattering gangways, one forward, another aft. A train awaited us, an old, narrow-gauge relic that disgorged a flume of sooty black smoke into the windless sky. We loaded into the coaches, straight-backed wooden seats, open windowed cars that had all the comfort of a stagecoach, our gear stuffed at our feet, the scent of age inside, like a musty basement.

The train started off with a jerk. A couple of the guys cursed. It took us out through the dock area, past a line of warehouses, into a switchyard, from there into the hills. At top speed we traveled about 20 miles per hour. Swaying and bucking, it took us through the dismal countryside, past small unpainted bamboo and cane houses with small windows, yards fenced to shield dormant gardens. Large fields were still being turned with single-bladed plows behind oxen. No sign of mechanization. Colors, gray, buff, and brown, occasionally a splash of green, some color near the houses. Trees wearing their winter foliage. Patches of snow crouching on the north facing hills.

During the trip a soldier came through with packets of mail, handed them out. I received a big packet. Many letters. I ripped some open and started reading as we snaked our way through the hills. It took us five hours to reach Camp Drake. No speed records were set. I just read and enjoyed my mail.

Camp Drake was a well-built Army camp with manicured grounds and concrete buildings. I was told that it was the "West Point" of the Japanese Army before World War II and was used by the occupation army after the war as a headquarters, then a replacement depot to supply troops and supplies to Korea. The barracks were clean and adequate with the assembly room close by. The mess hall was not much different than Fort Lewis or Fort Lawton—big, unhurried, with good food. Orders for the day were posted and read daily at 06:00. Our training schedule would allow us to get to Korea without delay, within 24 to 48 hours.

We began our processing the very next day. We were up at 06:00 and ready for our first formation at 08:00 at the reception center where we received our record jacket. We were informed that we would go to Korea via ship and that the training at Camp Drake would consist of nothing more than firing a few rounds. We would go as infantry, an order that didn't sit well with me. My objections weren't even heard.

I then went through a pay line and received a partial advance of $20 in script, not U.S. currency. Script was much like Monopoly money. The denominations went up to $10. It was the only means of exchange. Until then I had only 20 cents in my pocket. In the next line they reviewed my shots, found that I had been adequately punctured. I was given a copy of my record to carry with me. Another copy was added to my service jacket. I then went to the canteen, serviced by the Red Cross, and had a free cup of coffee and a donut. There, I also arranged to send a cable to Florence with a different group of volunteers, the "Army Officers' Wives' Club", a group of women whose husbands were in Korea. They talked with the GIs to give them moral support or write letters for them. I was able to get a supply of paper and envelopes at no cost.

From that big arena we went to another building where the soldiers without insurance or allotments could seek advice. We had another chance to exchange U.S. money for script. Then it was back to the barracks in the rain to await the noon chow call. It had rained hard all day, a steady downpour. There was no drainage system on the base. The water just kept accumulating in the low spots. Small lakes formed throughout the camp.

That afternoon we waited again, to be transported to the rifle range where we would fire our five shots. It was so wet they canceled the training. The range was flooded. They gave us the afternoon off and a PX ration card. I went to the PX with a couple of my buddies, hoping to find a gift for Florence. Unfortunately they had little to choose from in the way of gifts. I ended up buying silk pajamas, with robe and slippers, embroidered with colored thread,

Japanese in design, flimsy. I hoped to get it home before her birthday on December 20. They didn't sell birthday cards, only Christmas cards. It made me realize just how far apart in miles we really were.

I went to a movie that night at the most beautiful theater I have ever seen on a post. It was built like an old opera house, similar to the Radio City Theater in Minneapolis. But it had only one balcony. After the movie they had a stage show with Japanese actors, Kabuki dancers, samurai swordsmen. One of the men was tied up with rope, Houdini style, but through a series of contortions was able to remove his sword and cut himself free. Amazing. There was also a puppet show in which the puppets were actuated by long strings suspended from sticks. To finish it off, an octet of Japanese youths sang in their native language. Very good harmony. It was an evening well spent, a pleasant interlude from the usual hurry-up-and-wait existence of a soldier.

Two days later we received our marching orders, to embark on another troop ship, the U.S.S. *General Heintzleman*, destination Inchon, Korea. Before we left camp our names came out on orders for an early shipment. After that we had a physical examination, a short-arm inspection, where they checked everyone for VD, scabies and general health. After that we marched to the clothing warehouse that was secured behind iron bars to prevent the local residents from stealing. I received new clothing, new boots, five pairs of socks, new underwear, but no winter clothes other than our olive drabs and a jacket. I supposed warmer clothing would come once we reached our destination. After the clothing issue we had to roll our full field pack, consisting of a tent, tent pins, poles and two blankets, which are then bent in horseshoe fashion to fit over the backpack itself, which contains all the clothing you normally wear: underwear, fatigues, socks, personal items. Hung beneath this pack is a cargo bag which has the sleeping bag, poncho, towels and any extras. All combined, it weighed about 100 pounds, all on my back. And, oh, and I couldn't forget my best friend, the rifle.

We left camp at 10:00 on December 3 by way of a bus, to the same old, antiquated railroad that brought us in. The group that climbed into the cars that morning were considered the advance group. I was stuck in the KP department. It was the usual hurry up affair, pack 'em in, scoot 'em out, line 'em up.

The troop ship awaiting us at the pier was much the same as the *Freeman*, except that it had more room for troops, was painted battle gray, and appeared much more warlike. As I walked down the pier toward the forward gangway, the ship was a stark reminder of where I was and what I was expected to do. This was to be the last leg of our voyage. The next time we set our feet on land, we would be in a war zone. Days after that I could be on the front lines. The thought was enough to send a shiver down my back.

The man behind me grumbled as we approached the gangway. I turned, looked at him. He was smaller than me, about five-eight in height, appeared to be younger by a year or two. His face was half hidden beneath his helmet. I asked him where he was from.

He said he was from Fond du Lac, Wisconsin, that he got called up just when he was about to start a new job. I told him I was one up on him, that I'd been dragged away eight days after I was married.

The kid shrugged, obviously glad he wasn't in my shoes. I didn't hear his answer. His voice trailed off as I grabbed the rail. It was the last time I saw the soldier from Fond du Lac.

Ahead, a stream of guys were filing up the gangway, the long brown line, slow and plodding beneath their burdens. I was assigned to the 25th Division, and was told I would get my assignment when we reached Inchon on December 7, nine years to the day after the bombing of Pearl Harbor. I was sure I would be in the artillery, because our entire group was all F.A. I was split away from most of the boys, except my bunky and the lumberjack from Black Duck, Minnesota. We were told that we would go ashore in an LSI, because there were no useable docks at Inchon. Most of the harbor and the city was in ruins. We would be in tents at the Repo Depot before being moved to our assigned outfit.

George and Leonard came aboard. We were in the same division. Looked like we would stick it out together. Hoped we would all be on the same ship going home. Wrote my last letter before sailing. Learned we would have free postage in Korea.

The two-day crossing was uneventful. Lots of nervous tension. None of us had any idea of what to expect once we touched shore.

Frightened faces. Lots of letter writing. The guys stayed mostly to themselves. Deep thoughts. Longings.

I pulled KP, worked in the bakery, had a chance to sample all the fancy food that the GIs didn't see. Decided to eat good, knowing that K-rations would be our daily fare once we marched. I worked from 04:00 to 10:00. After that my time was free. I spent a lot of time in Melvin's compartment because they had good beds, two tables, and a head. My compartment had the typical canvas bunks.

It was cold on deck, a frigid wind across the iron-gray water, a dismal day to be going to war. The sky left no doubt that winter had descended on the Korean Peninsula, a country not much larger than Minnesota. Seoul lay on about the same latitude as Kansas City. It got very cold on the Great Plains. I assumed it would be the same in Korea.

I hoped they would issue us some warmer clothes.

5

BOOTS ON
THE GROUND

We arrived in Inchon on December 7, in the afternoon while the sun was still high. We were the only craft in the harbor, inching forward, toward the barren hills that showed no signs of buildings or people. It appeared to be a dead place. We could see no docks, no facilities, nowhere to tie up. Inchon's 11-foot vertical tide plane forced us to anchor far out. As we waited, we were given our "C" rations. Then I saw the LSI approaching to carry us ashore. The LSI was a huge craft, hollow at the middle, its marine engines in back, a huge, hinged steel door in front that dropped down to expel its cargo. After eating, we assembled by number, made our way to the side and climbed down the rope ladders draped from the side of the ship. We crowded into the LSI as more troops poured in. I was nervous and scared. No one talked. Everyone waited and shuffled until the boat was filled. Then it got underway.

We were dropped quite far out, on the mud flat. At Inchon, the rivers emptied into flat basins that formed the harbor, leaving one to five miles of slimy mud exposed at low tide. We sloshed out into water, then onto sand and rock and slime, the reeking spread of harbor bottom. Slowly, deliberately, line after line, we made our way ashore, stood on hard ground until our ranks were firmed. Nothing around us but desolation, broken equipment, scattered remnants, shattered structures, silence. I felt alone, even amid the ranks of men burdened beneath their packs. The longing for home was overwhelming, like a hunger inside. Everything was strange and unworldly, as if I had been dropped on another planet. One of the men beside me said, "Look at this shit hole. Why are we over here

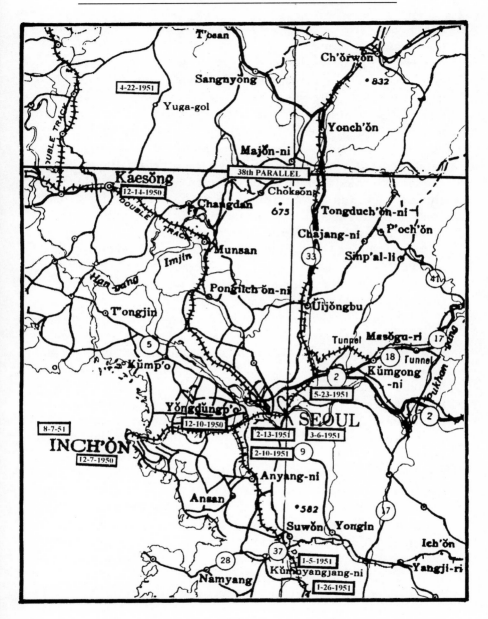

Locations of the 8th Field Artillery Battalion during the Police Action in Korea, 1950–1951 (map by Carleton Vang).

fighting for this?" A couple of the others nodded. My own convictions agreed. The lines moved forward, toward Inchon.

We were marched to a destroyed railroad yard. Blackened, burned, wreckage was scattered everywhere. Some of the rail lines had been blown. The Marines who had landed before us had left a path of destruction in their wake. Once we were assembled we were herded to an antiquated, crippled, filthy railroad car that would take us to the Replacement Depot in Yong-Dong-Po, about 20–30 miles away. We went by the numbers and boarded a car shattered by bullet holes, crowded into the small, cramped seats that held three men abreast, packed in our gear. There were no lights. A single dilapidated stove in the center of the car would have provided heat, had it been fueled. As it was, the car offered little protection from the wind that whipped across the railyard, carrying a stench that could only be described as the smell of war. We were given live ammo and told to keep our ears open for North Korean renegades, infiltrators that still roamed the area in search of supplies and food.

We stayed on the train all night, slept intermittently, heard aircraft overhead, recurrent noises outside that caused me to jump. It was frightening in the darkness, men shifting, going outside to urinate, to grab a smoke. I wondered where all this would take me. Nothing had prepared me for that night. I did not feel like an avenging soldier, intent on destroying an enemy. I felt instead like someone abandoned, pushed aside at the whims of others, into a land where every sound, every movement, brought a fear unlike any I had known.

We awoke early the next morning to a warm sun. The bright new day gave everything a new dimension. Even the wreckage seemed less ominous. There was movement in the yard. Workers plodded slowly toward their jobs. Trains moved at a snail's pace. We ate our rations, stood outside in the fresh air. About 30 men took off to explore the devastation. They were called back by the shrill sound of the train whistle. We loaded up again, left about 10:00.

We traveled about 20 miles, a very slow trip. Every town had a spur line that had to be cleared so we could gain the right-of-way. Each time our train stopped we were swarmed with kids of every age calling "Chow-chow-Joe," arms reaching, faces pleading, hunger in their eyes, begging for food, young boys, girls, some with smaller children tied at their waists, looking very much like the refuse of war. I could not refuse them. I emptied all the extra food I was carrying, candy, sugar, coffee, anything I could do without. Later that morning, we slipped into Yong-Dong-Po.

We had all that afternoon to find a new berthing place. The car we arrived in was packed. I and several others wanted relief from the crowd. The men I was with were a varied lot, all from the 6th Repo in Fort Lewis. My bunky was the shortest of the bunch, was well built, a born comedian. The Lumberjack was tall and lanky, a hometown guy from Black Duck, Minnesota. He hunted, cut pulpwood back home, lived in the woods, knew about the value of ammunition. Mr. Fixit, from Detroit, was plump, dreary-eyed. He was a mechanical genius who could fix anything. I had no special skills, except to take advantage of their collective genius. It was the Lumberjack who made the first suggestion, following a brief inspection of the cars we were connected to. His idea was to hole up in the baggage car, on top of the sacks.

It sounded like a good idea. We climbed in, all except our friend from Detroit. He began probing through the rain yard, looking for other things we could use.

We made ourselves comfortable on the sacks until our jack-of-all-trades came back. He said he'd found an old stove in another train, and needed help to lug it back. The prospect of heat sounded good to all of us. We followed him across the tracks.

Two of us carried the old stove while Mr. Fixit tore out the stovepipes and hustled them back in his arms. He was excited once we had everything inside. He was confident he could make the old relic work, and proceeded to poke a hole in the roof of the baggage car.

It took about a half hour to install the stove. My ship bunky and I had scrounged the area for wood; found most of it from a shattered railroad car. By the time we returned, Mr. Fixit had a small fire going. That afternoon we heated our "C" rations. We were comfortable and warm when the train moved out.

We arrived at the old 7th Division Camp south of Seoul and were immediately told we would move on line the following day. The camp had been trashed when the North Koreans retreated. There were no windows in the buildings. Many were destroyed. There were numerous bullet holes in the one to which we were assigned. Two stoves inside kept us fairly warm. Local water was not allowed, except by ration from the nearby water-treatment plant that was controlled by the Corps of Engineers. It had lots of chlorine in it, but not enough to make us sick.

When I crawled into my bag that night there were 20 men in our barracks. When I awoke the following morning there were about 150, jammed in, head to foot, like cordwood. The Lumberjack was the first to greet me upon awakening. He said he tried to wake me up during the night, but couldn't. He said jokingly he thought I had died. He said one of the barracks down the line burned to the ground. It was one helluva bonfire. Some claimed that infiltrators lit it. The guys who were displaced crowded into our barracks. I had slept through it all. By the time I saw the barracks, it was nothing but ashes. I didn't care. It was the first full night's sleep I'd had since leaving the States.

On Sunday, December 10, we were all packed and ready to go on line. Our destination was still a mystery. I had my MOS, 2704, and was assigned to a headquarters battery. I was separated from most of my buddies, who all got fair assignments in a recon unit. Jack would go with them. We had mail call. I got three letters, the greatest thrill a serviceman could have. Letters from home were like gold, treasured. We appreciated the fact that the Army did everything possible to get the mail to us, wherever we were.

On the day we moved out, the weather was warm, a full sun, mild breeze. The flyboys were putting on a show, sorties all day long. Mustangs screaming overhead. There was always a roar in the air.

The war didn't sound good. We were told the Eighth Army had formed a defensive perimeter just below the 38th parallel, north and east of Seoul, and that an uneasy stillness hung over the battleground. Chinese reinforcements were pouring in to strengthen their lines. Thousands of refugees were fleeing the capitol city. It was estimated that North Korean divisions numbered 150,000 men. That did not include the 28 Chinese divisions that had joined the fight. To counteract the threat, United Nations replacements were being brought in every day. A Dutch battalion had arrived, as had artillerymen from New Zealand and infantry battalions from Greece, Canada and France. The Turks were there. Enough, we hoped, to hold back the enemy. Our defensive positions stretched all the way from the Yellow Sea to the Sea of Japan. We hoped the battleline would hold at the 38th parallel. Perhaps then the power lords could start talking cease fire.

We got our shoepacks, heavy rubber boots with two quarter-inch felt inner liners, one pair of which was kept in the boot, another pair on our belt to dry out. We had to have a dry inner liner at all times to keep our feet protected and warm so we didn't get frost-bite. We were also issued heavy socks, but no mountain bags or wool caps. With our incomplete winter gear, we moved north toward Kaesong.

The convoy consisted of two open top 6 × 6 trucks, loaded with men, shoulder to shoulder on the hard steel platforms, one row facing the other. The roads were terrible, broken and rutted, gravel for a topping, like an old country road back home, but worse. We jostled along slowly, hoping to make the 46 miles to Kaesong before dark. Unfortunately, the sun set long before we arrived and we were forced to lean on our rifles for support while the trucks ground along the narrow road over the bone-jarring ruts that damn near snapped our necks. What a forlorn bunch we were, gazing most of the time at the floor of the truck, hopelessly alone in the khaki herd, catching someone else's glance now and then, not bothering to communicate. Occasionally, whenever we struck a rut, someone swore, cursing the Chinese. The guy beside me was smoking Chesterfields. The smoke went right up my nose, made me cough. I told him to put it out. He told me to mind my own business, that smoking was the only privilege he had left, if I didn't like it I could walk. I kept my mouth shut and looked at the deck. When darkness came I was in a state of half-sleep, nodding against my rifle, allowing my body to sway with the constant movement.

A grinding noise jolted me. Our truck skidded to a stop, slamming us forward. A guy in front stood up and peered over the cab. The rest of us grabbed our rifles. The truck ahead of us had flipped over.

We all jammed forward, peered over the side, saw the 6 × 6 lying in a depression, its wheels pointing skyward, still spinning. Men were lying all over the place, some moving, others crawling. Some were yelling. I heard a muffled scream. The headlights from our truck illuminated the scene. Some of the men in our truck jumped out. An officer came running, waving his hands, shouted that we were to stay where we were, that they didn't need any assistance.

Someone asked if they were going to right the truck. Negative! The officer said some of the men were going to crowd in with us, that we only have a few more miles to go. Then the truck would return to get the others.

We took our seats again, packed even tighter as we descended the small grade, saw the bridge that had been demolished, forcing us to take the bypass on a section of pontoons put down by the Engineers. We arrived in the Kaesong area about a half hour later. The total trip of 46 miles had taken us five hours.

We were encamped that night south of the city, in a dry riverbed. We pitched our tents, slept fitfully to await the dawn. It was the first night we heard the grumbling of artillery, like distant thunder. It kept me on edge. War suddenly took on an entirely new meaning.

We were rustled up at daylight, packed hurriedly, were loaded up. Took the same road south, past the bridge, the upturned truck, spent most of the morning traveling to a high valley just above Seoul, where we set up camp again. We stayed in Service Battery because Headquarters Battery had been split. We were extras, waiting to be assigned, moving to keep us away from the advancing Chinese. From our new camp we could see Seoul, a low, sprawling city that looked more like a dumpsite than a place for human habitation. A gritty smoke pall hung over the buildings. Above us the clouds came in, hovering over the trees. We were a stone's throw below the treeline, on a barren slope laced with scrub brush and boulders. We were told we'd be there for several days. No one knew for sure. It all depended on the enemy. We were always prepared to move.

I wrote home as much as possible, though it was limited because of our readiness. We searched daily for diversions because we were doing nothing. One day someone came up to me, told me to get my rifle. We were going to have a little target practice.

I followed the four guys to a small ravine. One of them pointed out our targets, a dozen empty cans on the opposite bank. The competition was simple. The first guy to get one to the bottom of the slope won the honor of being the luckiest shot. It was obvious the Army wasn't going to give us a sharpshooter medal for shooting at cans.

I slammed a clip into my rifle, picked out a can, fired a round. Missed.

The third kid over fired, sent a can spinning. It spiraled and rolled down the embankment.

I zeroed in my sights, kept firing the carbine until I hit my can once. I never was a good shot. That day I hoped I'd never have to use my rifle in combat. I didn't know what I'd do if I ever had to fire at a man. The thought alone was enough to paralyze me for an instant.

Heard big guns in the distance again, their booming low and distinct. Return fire going overhead, the hollow whistle of projectiles from .155 howitzers. Aircraft on a constant prowl. Movement on the roads below. Troops and trucks going east. A fire in Seoul. Black smoke rising in a lazy pattern, carried away by the wind. I watched it all with amazement, as if they were scenes from a movie. Still hard to believe that I was in the middle of a war.

A small Korean village was within sight of our camp. It didn't take long for the locals to appear with their hands outstretched. One, a middle-aged man who walked with a limp, came to us one day offering his help. He spoke limited English, but was able to get his point across with the help of gestures. He would get us straw for our bedding. I nodded, pushed him on his way.

He ambled off, returned in about a half hour with another smaller boy loaded down with a sackful of straw over his shoulder. In payment, I gave him a can of tomato puree. He was very grateful. He made it clear in broken English, while tugging at my shirt-sleeve, that he would also do our laundry. I took a dirty pair of olive drabs from my pack, shoved them into his hands. Grinning, he replied that his Mama-san would do the work.

He went off again, returned them before the end of the day, cleaned and folded. I gave him a couple of cigarettes and some candy.

He left with more business from the other boys. I turned in early. It was my night for a four-hour watch on outpost guard, on the lookout for infiltrators.

Guard duty gave me plenty of time to think, to wonder about the outcome of the war and to pause for memories. Before I went on that night there was rumor of our outfit going back to Japan if the Chinese kept advancing. Hearsay? No one knew. Some men were worried that we'd be pushed into Inchon harbor, unable to find passage, that we'd be placed under bombardment. It was rumored that the enemy had us outnumbered twenty to one. It was enough to make night guard a frightening experience. Every sound, every motion, sent a chill down my spine. I couldn't help but reflect on our inability to stop the Chinese advance. I heard the officers say that if we had a declared war with the Chinese we could then bomb their supply lines in Manchuria. But we hadn't declared war on anyone. We were merely in a defensive police action. General MacArthur was insistent on going across the border to attack their supply lines but good old Harry Truman prevented him from doing so. Our attacks were limited to targets south of the Yalu River. What a war. Sometimes it seemed we had our hands tied behind our backs, that we were fighting an enemy on their terms and not ours. But I realized that I was a soldier, and like the others, I had a job to do. I would face whatever came my way. Duty was something I had always taken seriously.

We were still in a rear area holding position on December 15, ten days before Christmas. We didn't do much except wait, pull guard duty, sit around and talk, play cards. We had little or no schedule for daily work except to keep equipment and rifles clean, to remain ready. I shaved and cleaned up for the first time in a couple of days. Sent my fatigues in with a young boy to be washed. He brought them back cleaned and folded, waited for his "chop-chop." I gave him one can of tomato puree. He was happy with that.

Late in the day a contingent of ROK came into the camp. They spent part of the afternoon digging a trench on the side of the hill. We didn't know what it was for. Some guessed it was for a latrine. Others said it was defensive. We hoped the Chinese weren't closing in. There was a lot of air activity. We couldn't get a word out of our officers. They ignored the ROK and went about their own work.

That night I had a fire on watch, a perk of sorts. Warmth from a 55-gallon drum. I burned everything I could get my hands on—paper, discarded clothing, wood scraps, dry grass. It helped ease the cold. It was late December, and winter was closing in fast. My breath was clearly visible in the cold air.

I awoke early the next morning to the sound of shouting. I peered out of my tent to see the ROK bringing in lines of prisoners, men tied together with ropes, wrist to wrist. They led them in small groups, sat them down near the trench they had dug, stood watch over them. Everything was quiet until after breakfast. Then it started.

I was just finishing my meal when the first volley rang out. A bunch of us bolted, then realized the firing was coming from the hillside, where the ROKs were. We were beginning to scatter when one of the GIs came rushing toward us. He was screaming. They were shooting the prisoners, lining them up, shooting them in the head.

We came out of the large tent and dashed toward the hillside. From where we were, we could see a line of men shoveling dirt into the trench. Behind them, a line of riflemen stood waiting. It was obvious that they were burying the dead.

My eyes were riveted on the sight. I couldn't believe what was happening. Condemned men covering up their dead? It took me only a second to realize that the shovelers were the next ones to be slaughtered. As I watched, one of the ROK came up and shouted at them. They dropped their shovels and stood with their backs to the riflemen. There were twelve of them, small men mostly, scantily clothed. None of them looked at one another. Two of them looked at us. Their mouths were tight, their bodies tense. The officer shouted a command. The rifles came up. At the instant they fired, the men drifted forward, some pulling others with them like a line of dominoes, falling into the pit. I could feel my breakfast starting to rise into my throat.

One of our guys shouted angrily, told them they had no right to shoot prisoners. The ROK officer swung on him, anger firing his eyes. "They are traitors!" he shouted.

By this time another group was shoveling, burying those who had fallen before them. It seemed as though they were hurrying their own execution. They worked fast under the spiteful shouts of their captors.

We moved closer. By this time there were about thirty of us, all in a group. The ROK officer tried to wave us away. He kept shouting in Korean, words we couldn't understand, trying to make it clear that this was their matter and that we were interfering. One of our boys yelled at them, to no avail. Then he turned and ran to get an officer.

Two other men broke away, started running back toward the camp. They were halfway to the tents when the third row of men were shot, a crisp volley, POP, POP, POP. I was so close I saw the blood spurt from their bodies, saw them spin and tumble into the trench, some still moving, twitching, an arm in the air, fingers opening, closing. Immediately another group began covering them with dirt. I saw some of them twitching. They weren't even dead. Yet they were being covered up.

I looked back, knowing I had to do something, saw a group of GIs headed toward the trench. Two of them wore bars. When they saw what was happening, they broke into a run. They ran right past us, directly to the ROK officer who was herding another group forward. All in all, there had been about 40 prisoners. Half of them already lay dead in the trench.

Our officer screamed directly in the ROK's face, his face livid with anger. He wanted an explanation, and he wanted it fast. The ROK pointed to the line of dead. Again he said something about traitors. He continued ordering his men. Those with the rifles appeared confused. A couple of them quartered their arms. The prisoners who were tied together huddled together in a group. Many of them were barefooted. A few were bleeding. One had blood frozen to his arm.

Our officer was vehement. He insisted that they leave, that they take their prisoners elsewhere. The ROK officer shouted something about this being their land, their problem, their solution. He was not intimidated when told that they were in violation of the Geneva Convention, that they could not shoot prisoners. The ROK officer was unmoved. These men were traitors, not prisoners. He had every right to execute them.

Our officer turned to us, told us to get back to our tents. He motioned to his aide, told him to get our names, ranks, and serial numbers in case we needed to testify at a later date. He was determined to end the executions.

We returned to our tents as the officer continued his shouting match with the ROK officer. In the end the firing squad and the prisoners were driven away in trucks. We didn't know where they went. Perhaps the remaining prisoners were shot somewhere else.

The dead men in the trench were covered up. Before the end of the day nothing remained to indicate they were there, except for a simple wooden cross someone had fashioned from remnants of an ammo box.

It was very obvious that an incident like that was the very reason we were not allowed to carry cameras with us into combat. No one really explained why we couldn't have cameras. We just followed orders. Even those who did manage to smuggle cameras in and sent film home said the pictures received had all been black. It was evident that the Army was X-raying any film that was sent back to the U.S. Pictures of prisoners being shot would cause a big ruckus with the high brass. Executions were not condoned, though they did occur. The ROK were not big on forgiveness.

On the 16th of December it began snowing. Large wet flakes coated the ground, began to pile up at noon, turned everything white, took away the stark grayness of the land. I welcomed the snow. It made our surroundings look like Minnesota. It covered up the makeshift grave, made me forget the horror of the executions.

In the afternoon the supply sergeant had us remove a squad tent from his truck. About eight of us grabbed it and put it up. It was a very large tent, about 12 × 20 feet in size, with lots of room inside. About 15 of us were quartered there. From somewhere, an oil stove appeared. We had heat and plenty of room and electric lights powered by a generator.

Supplies came in. I received my first pair of wool gloves, but no cap. Late in the day someone came up with the idea of making ice cream. We took some evaporated milk, sugar, and snow, mixed it in our canteen cups and stirred like hell. It took a while but eventually it thickened. It was almost like ice cream. We didn't do anything more except carry supplies. We had cut down a tree, but with the oil stove blazing, we didn't need the wood.

Sunday. No chaplain. Prayed by myself, off alone in the snow. The only sound was in the air. Planes overhead again, high up. The ground a peaceful white.

That afternoon a local Korean came into the camp offering to cut hair. He had scissors with him, made a clip, clip sound with it. He was middle-aged, wore a quilted jacket, black pants. Had a long, narrow beard that hung on his chin like floss. We paid him with a pack of cigarettes or tomato puree, his choice. He sharpened his razor on his belt, all six inches of it. While he was cutting the sergeant's hair, I sat nearby, awaiting my turn, dozing on an empty crate.

Suddenly the sergeant leaped off his box, swung around and caught the barber on the side of his face with a clenched fist. I opened my eyes in time to see the Korean fall to the floor. The sergeant stood over him, shouting, kicking at his hand. Out fell a packet of bills. The Korean had slipped $85 out of his back pocket.

Angered to the point of fury, the sergeant kicked him in the side. The Korean rolled over, tried to get to his feet, sprawled. The sergeant kicked him in the butt, propelling him forward on his face.

The sergeant screamed, swore a stream of obscenities, kicked him again, reached down and yanked him to his feet. The Korean was no match for the sergeant, who was about twice his size. He took a punch directly in the face. Blood squirted from his nose. He went down again, rolled over. The sergeant kicked him viciously, his heavy combat boot crunching against his side. Grunting, the Korean made a dash for the tent flap. He only made it part way. Someone tripped him, sent him sprawling. Again, the sergeant was on him, kicking, beating until someone pulled him off.

Trust and honesty were not apparent morals in Korea. The desperate, displaced people took what they could, robbing, stealing, commandeering anything in order to survive. But the barber need only have asked for food. It would have been given to him. There had been no need to steal from a GI. The bloodied barber was taken to the locals down in the village and turned over to the police, where his punishment would undoubtedly continue. Perhaps he would be one of the next to be tied wrist-to-wrist and led to a trench. We never saw him again.

Cold on Monday. Some of the vehicles wouldn't turn over and had to be jump-started or pulled. We eventually got them all going. Living outside began to get miserable. What we really needed was a field kitchen, some way to heat our rations. One hot meal a day would have been welcomed. Our daily rations, beside the food, consisted of the usual "C" assortment, some candy, a pack of cigarettes, toilet paper. That day I received a Tootsie Roll.

The British moved in nearby, close enough so we could see them, hear them. They were a jolly bunch of fellows, all reservists waiting like I was to return home. The British require 12 years of service from everyone, two years active duty, ten years reserve.

One morning I heard a loud commotion in the British camp. The men were beating on cans, pipes, vehicles, anything they could get their hands on. Laughter came out in a roar. One among them was shouting, angry, stomping from man to man, lashing out at them. We learned later that he was the sergeant major who was extremely proud of the long, waxed handlebar mustache he had groomed. On that day someone had entered his tent and had clipped off half the mustache. His anger, and the resulting catcalls, created a furor in the camp. I think the British laughed all day.

We learned early on that the British received a rum ration every day and that some among them didn't drink. They did, however, have a passion for American Old Gold cigarettes. Trading Old Golds for rum was a daily routine.

We were up early the next day. The British had already left. At 08:30 we loaded our truck with the tents, poles, other equipment. The Chinese were on the move again. Lots of detonations north of us, that deep, hollow pounding that was like a constant headache. All that day we headed south, ended up near Young-Dong-Po again, very close to the camp we occupied when we came inland from Inchon. We put up the big tent, found a second stove. We were very comfortable. I found a floor mat in an abandoned house. It was about two inches thick, three by six feet in size, soft and well made. I placed it beneath my bag, laid down about 20:30 that night, slept until dawn. It was the first warm night since we had moved north. I was still in Service Battery, doing nothing but guard duty.

I saw our first squadron of jet fighters headed north: F-86 Sabres. They were new on-line. Obviously the brass had strengthened the air force. We hoped the added airpower would soon turn the tide of battle in our favor.

We moved again the following day, north, up the same rutted roads, through the packed snow. Lines of infantry slogging with us. Tanks off in the distance. Going toward the front.

Another guy and I were reassigned to Headquarters Battery again, to replace two corporals who were sent back to Service Battery for a rest. We ended up ten miles south of Kaesong, wondering if the Chinese would cross the 38th parallel into South Korea. All I did was pull guard duty. When the rest of the boys came up, our unit comprised the 24 hour outpost guard, walking the line at night, stealthily, no fires, no talking. Scary as hell whenever someone moved. The enemy wore no identifiable uniforms, nor did many of the ROK. It was difficult to tell them apart. Lots of action over the far hills. I could see star shells bursting up high in the distance, to help the spotters select targets. Heard the growl of artillery, like an ogre clearing its throat. We were always in fear of an all out Chinese offensive.

On December 24 we slept in a shattered town that had been vacated by force. All the civilian population had become refugees, mingling with the thousands of others that had moved south with whatever belongings they could carry. Three of us put up in a one-room house constructed on four upright posts, one on each corner. The posts supported the ceiling beams. The walls were made of mud plaster, straw and clay combined. The roof was thatch, high pitched to drain off the rain. The space inside was about twelve feet square. We built a fire outside next to the wall, in the grubbed-out cooking hole. The ingenious system allowed heat from the fire to travel through a narrow tunnel flume beneath the room's three-inch floor. In passing, the smoke heated the floor, then exhausted on the opposite side of the house. We slept across the tunnel. One night it got so hot I crawled out of my sack and slept on top to protect myself from the hot floor. One of the boys got his billet so hot his sack started to smoke. Tending the fire was a careful and deliberate task. I expected that the Koreans had the heating system all figured out. We, of course, being unfamiliar with primitive living, had to learn by experience.

I found a shower unit nearby, in the 2nd Division. I was fortunate enough to use it. Washed off the mud and felt clean again. Never had a shower felt so good.

I was now in Headquarters Battery, FDC section, doing what I had been trained to do at Fort Sill, the only difference being this was not a school problem, but the real thing. A mental adjustment was needed. The forward observers had real targets, and it was our job to help take them out.

Positioning of the guns was vital to our success. Whenever a general location for each howitzer was found, the 6 × 6 truck pulling the piece was directed to its location. The gun was then disconnected from the truck. The spreader bars were extended and dug in because they supplied the foundation, assuring that the piece wouldn't move when fired. This had to be done for each of the six guns. Ammunition was then unloaded and prepared for firing. As soon as the guns were fixed, the report was given "ready to fire."

The first essential prelude to firing was to establish "base point registration" which was a specific target identified by the Forward Observer. This consisted of firing one round for general location and then adjusting the trajectory with add or subtract commands or left or right commands, until a good steady bracket was accomplished and the term "fire for effect" was given. This exercise was repeated for each gun battery until they attained a stable fix on the target.

Each gun had an aiming scope that was focused on a stake about 25 yards from the gun. When the gunner heard the command from FDC to go left or right so many degrees, he turned a wheel that rotated the gun right or left, away from the aiming stake. When the command came in to raise or lower by degrees, the gunner changed the angle of fire accordingly and reported the gun ready. The officer or chief of section then gave the order "fire two rounds." Before the gun sighting changed, the crew of six was told to ready the charge, the fuse and the number of rounds for firing.

The gun crews were families. They lived together, ate together, slept together. They dug the gun into place, constructed shelters, acquired a way to heat the shelters and in general, existed as one. It was a very competitive arrangement. The speed in which a crew could get "ready to fire" was a matter of pride. The speed a crew could achieve from firing to travel was also important. When they fired as a unit, all guns fired as one. When they traveled as a group, they looked like a bunch of gypsies. I saw rugs from shelters draped over guns, and 55-gallon drums that had been made into stoves swinging from the ends of gun barrels. They carried everything they needed to make it easier to construct a shelter at the next location— crates, boxes, sandbags. A 6 × 6 pulled each gun. The crew of six rode in back. Other vehicles were necessary to carry the additional support groups, such as supply and FDC.

When we were on the move it was our job to go from traveling to firing as fast as possible. Sometimes we made the transition in as little as five minutes.

The base point registration procedure was done every time we moved and set up. It often involved only one gun battery if it was a short-stay situation. Without a "base point registration" for each battery there was no way to have the battery or battalion fire as one unit. When a battery fired one round it was, in reality, six rounds at the same target point or eighteen rounds at one target if the battalion fired as a unit. Since target acquisition was being done by radio, the radio operator was a very important person because he had to receive and relay the commands accurately and quickly. When telephone line communication was established and headsets were activated, radio congestion was relieved.

A typical FDC set up consisted of position one, my job, working at the plotting table as the horizontal control officer. My plotting table received commands from the FO and converted them to changes left or right, adding or subtracting yards.

My work was done by placing a blank sheet of paper on the plotting board, the top being hypothetical north, the bottom south. I then placed three pins near the bottom of the paper, in a row, each pin signifying a battery, A, B, or C. I would then take a "fan," a plastic device so called because it resembled a small fan, with deflection changes indicated on top by degrees, yard marks on the side and a notch at the bottom. I would secure one fan to each of the pins at the notch. These would then be adjusted as needed when firing information came in from the FO. A situation map for our particular location was always secured to the plotting board. It was always the same map held by the FO.

The forward observer would begin the process by giving his azimuth to the target or intersection coordinates from the situation map. The map had all coordinates of the area clearly defined: railroads, roads, intersections, villages, hills, etc. Hills were identified by elevation. A hill 651 feet above sea level would be identified as Hill 651.

The FO would give a compass reading from his location to the identified target, as if he were the firing piece, either A, B, or C, on the plotting board. I then pinned the center of a firing disc on the location where he wanted the round to land. The firing disc, or aiming circle, was a round piece of paper divided into squares, representing yards, marked with a north, south, east, west grid. We would then position the firing disc to the given compass direction of his sight line, his compass reading, aligning it north-south. I would then inform the VCO operator (Vertical Control Officer) the number of yards to target. We would then fire a single round.

When the FO saw the initial burst, he would then respond with yard adjustments. We would move the pin in the disc according to his instructions and give a new deflection and elevation for the next round. This procedure was repeated until all guns in each of the batteries were zeroed in on the base point.

Once the base point had been fixed, all further adjustments were made from it. From that point on, accuracy was dependent upon the skill and proficiency of each gun crew.

Position Two was taken up by Sefton Stallard. As vertical control officer, he charted the add/subtract orders to change gun elevations.

Position Three was the S-2 Intelligence Officer. This officer was in charge of the current local map of the firing area with the prearranged and designated targets. This map showed the front lines and the minimum no-fire line. The chart person was generally the ranking NCO or Officer of the Day. Position Three was the communications center, the receiving point of all incoming telephone or radio communications. Outfitted with headsets and microphones, this position received very little cross talk while firing. He was responsible for each of the six guns in a battery.

Position Four was the S-3 Officer, who was in charge of the firing. Our Captain Joe was responsible for allocating the amount of fire on a target for each of the 18 guns. He was the boss. No questions asked.

In an ideal or full-blown situation we were supposed to have one HCO (Horizontal Control Operator) table and three VCO (Vertical Control Operator) stations with people at each who could take adjustments from the HCO table and transmit them to each gun battery.

When we were stationary, the fire direction center had to be set up and be able to receive communications from the forward observers. These communications first came by radio. In fact many times our radio operator would tell us that he had a radio contact with a FO while we were moving. He had to tell him we were moving and were unable to accept his request for artillery support. When we stopped traveling and were prepared to receive requests from the FO, the requests started with the two words "fire mission." This was always received in a "high alert" attitude. Everyone on duty prepared to do their job. The first thing was to receive the location of the target, the concentration and the amount of support required. The officer on duty was in charge of alerting the proper number of gun batteries. It was our responsibility to make the calculations to get one round on the way immediately so that the FO could call back an adjustment. This process was repeated using one howitzer by bracketing the target until the FO was satisfied that he had the correct range. Then the command would come, "fire for effect." At this point the officer would step in and command the number of rounds from each gun for effect. Generally it would be three, or in some extreme cases, five rounds.

The 105 howitzer fired a 105mm shell (4.5 inches approximately) with a range from 3,000 yards to 11,000 yards. Each shell was in two pieces near the gun, the powder casing containing seven powder bags (called charges) and the warhead. The warhead could be high explosive (HE), the standard shell head that explodes on impact and spreads concussion and shrapnel as its destructive power, a white phosphorous (WP), a very hot burning substance that would create fires on people and buildings or whatever it came in contact with, a variable time (VT), a time fuse shell that was set to explode a number of seconds after firing. This was used whenever we wanted to have the shell explode twenty feet above the target. VTs were very effective when we were firing into trenches or bunkers. Time on target (TOT), was a procedure used to alert many different artillery units and also Navy support vessels to fire shells at a prearranged target, so that all shells, from ground and sea, arrived at the same time. This had a very effective panic result and was used occasionally to rout the enemy.

Ours was a twenty-four hour a day operation. We were always ready to fire upon command. The nice thing about being in FDC was that we were always in a heated, lighted environment, with a strong defense perimeter around us, relatively safe from attack.

Our driver was a short guy named Earl. He was from New Mexico and was part Mexican. He said the Army provided the first opportunity for him to sleep on a bed. It was just before Christmas that Earl came to us and said in all seriousness that he had to go home. His girlfriend was going to have a baby.

We looked at one another and tried to hold back our laughter. Finally someone reminded Earl that he'd been in Japan for two years, that it was impossible for his girlfriend to be pregnant. But Earl insisted that she was. She had told him in a letter.

I took Earl by the shoulder and pulled him closer, told him that it was not his baby, that someone else was the father. He insisted. She had told him he was the father.

I asked Earl if he knew about sex. He said he did, that they had laid together before he left to come overseas. The other boys tried their best to hold back their laughter.

I told him it took nine months to make a baby. If it was his, it would be a year old now. I explained that it was impossible for him to be its father.

He thought for a while, then shook his head, left the tent in a state of confusion. The laughter followed him outside.

Earl continued to get advice from his commanding officer and also from the chaplain. In the end, Earl understood. He never did go home.

On December 24, the North Koreans once again held claim to all territory north of the 38th parallel. On that same day, Lt. General Walton Walker was killed. He was traveling north from Seoul, on his way to present citations to two British and American units, when his Jeep collided with an ROK army truck. It was to be a turning point for the war, for it would herald the arrival of General Ridgeway.

On Christmas Day we had a turkey dinner with extra food, mashed potatoes, all the trimmings, the best the Army could put together. It was a small touch of home to an otherwise bleak existence, very much appreciated. After walking the chow line we all found a place to eat, on truck fenders, on boxes, the lucky ones in the cab. The officers had a tent, with tables and folding chairs and trays on which to eat, not mess kits. Christmas was a personal time for many. Remembrances of home were the topics of discussion. I remembered the tree, the many gifts, the table set with plentiful food, the laughter, church, time to be with God, our family all together. It was different in Korea. We ate outside in the cold, bundled in everything we owned. The food lost its heat before it reached our mouths.

We had no sooner eaten our turkey dinner when the march order came. Eat the meat and off your seat. We gotta get going.

When a march order came down we had to be on the move as quickly as possible. We took pride in the fact that we could change from a firing situation to a moving condition in less than one hour. This meant that 18 howitzers had to be changed from firing position to travel and hooked to a truck. Ammunition on the ground was loaded on the trucks or disposed of. All of the support groups such as communications, kitchen, medical, living, and service-associated personnel had to break down and move. It all happened fast and was well organized. Haste was imperative, in that it could, and did, save lives.

We all started to pack up and prepared to move. It was not a simple task. When the unit was stationary for a while, it was always harder than when we were on the move daily.

Stallard and the rest of us packed up the FDC equipment and our personal gear into the 6 × 6. We were all prepared to leave when Stallard turned to me and asked where Schranck was.

I looked around to where I thought he was. He wasn't in sight. I shouted his name as loud as I could. No reply. The truck was running. All our gear was stowed. The first vehicles were already underway. I hopped aboard, shouted again.

Then I heard him. We both turned in the direction of the shout, over near the wire section. Schranck came running toward our truck, a drumstick in one hand, and a jar of medical alcohol in the other, a jar he had bartered long and hard to obtain. He climbed aboard just as our truck was pulling out. He was all smiles.

Our convoy headed south, over the rough road out of Kaesong. It was a cold, clammy day. Heavy clouds to the north. Snow dusted with dirt. Sounds of gunfire closer than normal.

We slowed down through a small town filled with shattered buildings, broken equipment. It was there we saw a young boy, perhaps 8–10 years old. It was hard to tell his age, given his size and appearance. He was sitting on the side of the road, bundled in ragged clothing, staring at us as with a look that went beyond the present. He was the most forlorn boy I had ever seen, large eyes pleading, his mouth dirty from eating anything he could scrounge, his hair ragged, his feet covered with tattered sandals, his skin as dirty as the ground he sat on. We paused there for several minutes, wondered if he had been abandoned. If so, his parents were dead. He had nowhere to go, no home. I wondered what would happen to a kid like that. He'd end up in an orphanage or dead on the side of the road.

The truck lurched, then stopped again. In that moment I knew I had to do something to rescue the small lad from death. I leaped out of the truck and knelt at his side, said the words I hoped he would understand. "You come. Chop-chop." It took only a second for his eyes to light up. Without saying a word, he reached out for me.

I scooped the boy up in one arm and handed him to Stallard. I leaped in behind just as the truck moved forward. No one said anything. They hustled the boy forward and sat him down between them, began handing him food and chocolate. He ate like a famished beast.

"BOY-SAN," YOUNG KOREAN BOY—a street urchin was sitting on the curb in Kaesong, Korea, around Christmas time 1950, when the 8th Field Artillery Battalion and the entire 25th Infantry Division were retreating south. His value was important to our unit's safety because he could identify North Koreans for us. We took him into our unit and fed and purchased new clothes for him to wear. If we had not befriended this boy he most likely would have been a war casualty.

We called him "Boy-san" from that moment on He became a permanent part of our Corps. As we went south, he never spent much time in the FDC, but was closer to the wire section because they traveled from our area to the front, to the gun batteries and to Division, to connect everyone by telephone lines whenever we stopped. Boy-san wanted to be on the move. Soon the forward observers became aware of just how important he was to them. He could tell the difference between a North Korean, "N," and a South Korean, an "S." There were several times when he saved a GI's life because he could differentiate between the enemy and the ROK.

On December 26 General Matthew B. Ridgeway was appointed commander of the 8th Army in Korea. On that day we settled down again in another area south of Kaesong. Some of the boys began receiving packages, smaller ones that were not crushed or damaged. Bob Schranck received a big aluminum box. We all gathered around. I got some cookies. Someone else got a Nut Goodie.

We were all prepared for food. There was nothing like food from the States to make every man salivate. But as he lifted off the lid, we all sat back in dumb surprise. The box was filled with civilian clothes. Everybody started laughing. The package had been mailed to him at Fort Lewis after he wrote home informing them that no more enlisted reserves would be called overseas.

Bob put on a show. He dressed up in his plaid shirt and his new gabardine trousers, and paraded around the tent like a movie star, bowing to the hoots and hollers of the men. He put on quite a show. Of course, civilian clothes were not allowed or appreciated by the brass. Bob was told abruptly to get rid of the civvies or mail them back home. It was shortly after that we saw the old Papa-san wearing one of his shirts. Bob had given them to the Koreans.

Weather conditions remained raw and cold. The temperature hovered around 25 degrees during the day and zero at night, much the same as Minnesota. There was little snow on the ground, only patches covered with dust, frozen mud in places, crusts of ice over the snowmelt.

We had a short church service. The chaplain came up from Service Battery. He did not like the idea of going toward the action. He did his duty as ordered and then returned as quickly as he had come. I had no conversation with the chaplain. He was more suited for the rear, protected areas. For my religious needs, I relied on the small New Testament given to me by my church when I left St. Paul. It was a constant source of comfort.

It was well known that the Chinese were moving south, but had bogged down north of the 38th parallel because of their inability to service the troops. They lacked motorized vehicles, so all their supplies had to be brought in by horses, carts, or on the backs of their soldiers. Our situation map was updated daily and it was obvious that soon we would have to retreat. Although the enemy received maximum punishment day after day from both artillery and air strikes, we knew it was just a matter of time before they would begin their offensive. By the end of the year, the enemy had nearly a half million men waiting in the mountains. All they needed was a command to set them loose.

It was a tense time.

6

RETREAT

The final days of 1950 were somewhat casual. We had our usual duties, fired our batteries at targets identified by the forward observers.

When we moved into another small village on the 28th, we needed a place to stay, so we took over a small house, forcing its occupants to leave. The old Papa-san, a thin but firm individual, stood up to us rather well, insisting that he remain. He offered the services of his wife to take care of our clothing. She was a short, wrinkled lady with a flat face. He would stay and tend our fires, keep us warm, he said, and watch so we wouldn't burn his place down. They were good people, very pleasant, polite, always bowing. In their usual, humble Korean manner, they responded to our every need, without question, without complaint.

The house we occupied was firm, but the shacks nearby had been damaged and stripped for firewood. I wondered as I looked through the remnants of the village, where all the civilians had gone. Most of them had simply taken their belongings and walked away. Either we, or the Chinese, had forced them out. It was pitiful to see them leave, bundles on their shoulders, herding their children, heading south to take shelter anywhere they could find it. God, I hated war.

I received a box of useful items from home: a sewing kit, which I used to repair my beat-up jacket, and a fingernail kit to trim my blackened nails. That same day Stallard and I found an old tub, filled it with water, melted snow, added a small packet of powdered soap, and proceeded to boil our pants. We wrung them out, hung them up to dry inside the house. Most of the dirt had been removed. Clean clothes were a luxury.

I was on guard duty from 02:00 to 04:00. Tried to write a letter between answering the telephones and checking the radio. I had six telephones and three radios to attend in rather dim light. Most of the time I was alone. Sometimes an officer accompanied me, but that was seldom. They preferred sleeping to watch duty.

On the last day of the year, Bob Schranck and I brought out our Christmas cards and had a lot of fun comparing them. He had also received a deck of canasta cards in the aluminum box so we spent the day learning the game. Bob, who knew the rules, became the teacher.

The wire section was always the first to have lights after FDC obtained them. Generally, they also had head cover, a tent or a structure of some kind. So that's where we played. We used the side of a crate for a tabletop, cans and barrels for seats. We played most of that afternoon. Schranck, Stallard, RBH, Little Joe, and Frenchy joined in the game. It was the last time we would play cards for quite some time.

On January 1, 1951, the Chinese began their all-out offensive, and all hell broke loose.

It was our last day for "A" rations, fresh meat, potatoes, salad and fruit. The meat was Swiss steak. The gravy was juicy, well made, with a great aroma. It was the first "A" ration we had since leaving the ship, except for the turkey at Christmas.

That night, as darkness fell, the entire front line was illuminated in a barrage of intense mortar and artillery fire as the enemy struck south through the minefields and barbed wire entanglements. Their major effort was directed at the U.S. I and IX Corps situated above Seoul. It was obvious from the start that they were intent on re-taking the Capitol City.

We fired our last rounds that night, then prepared to retreat as the Chinese Army struck hard toward the rail center at Wonju. As it turned out, the only units escaping the full fury of the assault were us and the Turkish Brigade. We had time to pack up and run.

I awoke from what little sleep I had, only to find our room swathed in smoke and fumes. Hacking and coughing, I crawled out into the fresh air as fast as I could, found out that someone had fueled our kerosene heater inside the house with gasoline, creating toxic fumes. I gulped the cold air thinking that I could have died in the hut had I not been aroused by the commotion outside.

Everyone was moving. Trucks had been started. Men were shouting orders. Out on the road a convoy was forming. Stallard shook me out of my lethargy and shoved me toward one of the vehicles. His urgency was clear. The front line had come apart.

I could hear explosions in the distance, huge detonations, like an ammo dump going up. Aircraft were screaming toward the front. North Korean artillery was coming in, WHUMP, WHUMP, WHUMP, behind the hills that separated us from the enemy lines. I grabbed my stuff and threw it into the truck, stuffed my most recent letters into my jacket and started out with the convoy.

The 25th Division had landed in Korea on July 11, 1950. Since that day they had been in constant contact with the enemy. The 8th FA Battalion was the most decorated unit, along with the 27th Infantry Regiment, which we supported. We were known as the 27th Regimental Combat Team. It was a good outfit with proficient officers and seasoned enlisted men. They had fewer casualties than some of the other units in Korea. In fact, we in the ER were its first replacements, to bring it back to full strength. The unit had a very proud attitude. It was time again for the 8th to prove themselves in battle. It was certain that we'd have our work cut out for us as soon as we could establish a strong defensive perimeter.

We were in the convoy all afternoon. It was slow going. Massive amounts of men and material were moving south with us. The sky slagged with clouds. Civilians were on the road as well, Korean men and women, children, ragged, heads bent, slogging along with the trucks. Up ahead, the road was a black ribbon against the white snow. Exhaust fumes fogged the sky as the trucks labored forward. It wasn't long before we stopped and waited for the line to move again. Our truck was overloaded, too many men for the space, some standing, others with their legs dangling over the tailgate. As we waited, I jumped out, shouted to my crew. "I'm going to look for another ride. There's got to be more space somewhere."

Stallard leaped out with me, followed by Schrank. We walked forward down the road, peering into the loaded trucks, found nothing but packed soldiers and equipment. We kept looking. Soon we found what we wanted, an empty ambulance. We asked the driver if we could crawl inside. He agreed. It took us only seconds to jump in. What a break. The ambulance was heated. We had seats on both sides.

We moved into a village about five miles north of Seoul, where we set up our batteries to pound the approaching Chinese.

We took up residence in a hut occupied by a single Korean peasant. The Papa-san refused to move. Communicating with him was difficult, but we got his attention by making it appear like we were going to destroy his hut. He was quick to wave his arms, to say "No, no." Once he understood our intentions, we put him to work with our Korean cook. He was told to keep fires for hot water and us. He learned quickly how to take directions. We paid him a couple of cigarettes to maintain fires for four rooms.

We moved again the following day, south, to take up a better position to protect Seoul and the harbor at Inchon. South of us, the Army was evacuating the supply center at the ancient city of Suwon. To the west, at Kimpo Airfield, a half million gallons of fuel and napalm were burned to keep them from falling into enemy hands. A tremendous black cloud of smoke hung over the city like an evil apparition as all the military installations, once thought secure, were dynamited and burned.

The war was close now. I could see and hear it every day, on the ground, in the sky, in every dogged movement of the troops, in the officers' eyes, in their commands. Serious business. Lives on the line. We hurried instead of walked. Heard the rumble of guns on our heels, knew the gravity of our tasks. I trembled when the ambulances and the trucks drove past with wounded in their holds. I realized just how close the Chinese were when I heard the cackle of the 50mms.

Move. Set up. Fire. Break down. Move again. A steady, mind-numbing routine. Pour on the rounds. Ammunition kept coming in by truck to keep the guns firing. Line after line of vehicles grinding up from the south.

A brief pause now and then, knowing we would move again that night. The winter cold and dampness had nearly everyone coughing. My nose drained constantly. I wiped it away, only to have the mucus freeze on my gloves. I had a break one afternoon for a couple of hours. Used the time to heat some water and soak my feet clean, and put on the new socks I had received. It was a break to get clean, dry socks.

On January 3 we began moving out of Seoul. The Chinese had bolstered their divisions to the north, east, and west of the city. Their assault was imminent. Enemy columns had already broken through on the northern front. Buildings on the outskirts were aflame. A dark, incessant gout of smoke seemed to swallow the sky. Embers whipped by the wind were carried aloft by the firestorm. Civilians who had waited too long, hoping the city would be saved, began stumbling out with the retreating army, to escape the looters and ravaging bands of renegades.

On the 4th, we were in full retreat to the Han River. Behind us the city of Seoul fell into enemy hands for the second time, a sickening reminder that the war had changed. Fleeing elements clogged the road. Anything that could move on wheels or on foot attempted to keep pace with the army. I was in a truck, creeping along, my sense of haste kept alive by round after round of artillery raining down on the city and near our columns. On both sides of the truck, bedraggled lines of people slumped along under their burdens. Some people on the roadside were nothing more than ragged bundles. Others had given up, content to die where they sat, their belongings snatched up by those who needed what was discarded. Most had only the clothes on their backs. Children were wailing.

One mother fell ahead of our truck, on the side of the road. Her child rolled from her arms and lay on the road, blood on its head. One of the men in the rear of the truck was about to jump out and help, when an officer shouted for him to remain where he was.

The soldier's face was etched with concern. He asked about the baby. The officer was emphatic. He said to leave the baby where it was, that we had a war to fight. The soldier looked back to the road, where the baby lay. The mother had rolled aside, into the ditch. The baby lay by itself, bundled in rags.

He turned and took his seat, looked down at the bed of the truck. He muttered that it didn't seem right. The officer told him to forget what he saw, that he'd go crazy carrying those images with him. He needed to concentrate on his job, not on every Korean that fell to the side of the road.

The soldier hid his face in the folds of his jacket. But how could one forget a child laying in the road? How could one forget a dying mother? How could one forget the inhumanity of war when it was right in your face?

We came to the last pontoon bridge over the Han when the sun was low. By this time the Chinese artillery had zeroed in on the location. As we started across I heard the shells come in, saw them explode in the shallows where the ice had jammed up amid the flow of wreckage, watched them take out some of the people. Corpses in the water. Red patches of blood on the ice. Blooming explosions ripping through the mud. Gouges of earth spattering on the bridge. There were too many people. Some, who had tried wading through the freezing water, were swept away by the slow moving current. A truck lay aside the pontoons, overturned. The main bridge had been shattered, its spans angling crazily into the river. Whoosh! Whump! The shells came with regularity, one after the other, scattering the refugees, so many that they slowed down the retreat, stalled the vehicles on the pontoon bridge. Up ahead the GIs had to force them off so the trucks could move, following a line of tanks burdened with troops.

When we reached the south shore, our vehicle pulled up next to a truck, going in the other direction and hesitated in the slow traffic. It was there I saw a sight that almost brought tears of joy to my eyes. On the truck beside us was a winter sleeping bag, a mummy bag, rolled up, perched on the very top of the supplies. Having slept in a thin, inadequate summer bag for weeks, it was imperative that I take advantage of the situation. Leaning over, I snatched the bag from the truck and hugged it to my chest, as if it had just dropped down from heaven.

A call came from the back. Someone asked if I was going to rent the bag out. He offered to pay me $10 script for one night. Another said he'd give me $20. I rejected all offers.

It was very late when our unit pulled off the road. We set up the FDC immediately. The guns were positioned. Ammunition came up. We began firing at once, taking coordinates from the FOs as fast as they could send them. By early evening we were throwing everything we had at the Chinese, hoping to stem their advance. We didn't know where we were, only that it was somewhere near the ancient city of Suwon. We fired most of the night. I slept on my feet. All night long we poured in return fire. We fired until noon the next day.

We moved again, to a point south of Suwon, to a dry riverbed. We got there about 20:00. At that point I hadn't had my clothes off in ten days. I was caked with dirt. My body crawled beneath my clothing. After we set up the tent for the officers, I found a place beneath some bushes and rolled out my mummy bag. Inside I found a pair of pants, size 32, about 6 sizes too small. Whoever had the bag before was a small man. I slid into the bag, clothes and all, snuggled down, drew my head in and fell asleep.

When I awoke in the morning I was covered with snow and frost. Counting my new acquisition, I had a shelter half, three blankets, three summer bags, and a poncho, adequate enough for the Korean winter. I was in sleep heaven.

I was in Headquarters Battery with about 130 men, in a battalion of 700. One battery (the service battery) was quite far south of us. They brought in supplies daily. The 27th Infantry regiment was always in front of us for protection. They were known as the "Wolfhounds." We were known as "The Wolfhounds Bark," because of the artillery. Together we formed the 27th Regimental Combat Team of about 4,000 men. All that and three more RCT teams made up the 25th Division of about 18,000 men. The extra men came from the outfits not on line, such as finance, personnel, ordinance and so forth.

A typical move was scheduled after breakfast, before lunch, so we could be set up and be firing before dark in a new location. We moved into the rear area, into another small village situated in the hills. We stayed one night, then moved again, closer to the firing batteries and infantry to hunt out the Chinese. By this time large elements of the enemy had surged through a gap in the lines and were threatening us with a deeper penetration. We were in snow about a foot deep. Everything was white and blinding. We moved almost all the time, short distances, countering the attacks. Their shells were coming in steadily, carving up the area. They wanted to knock out our guns, as much as we wanted to knock out theirs. It was a seesaw game, accuracy being the key.

We were on "C" rations, eating out of cans. They were our daily staple until rations came up from the rear. The British boys were close by, supporting us. We got acquainted with them, drank some hot tea, traded cigarettes for some of their rum. We sure wished our cooks would make coffee and keep it hot like the Limeys kept their tea hot.

We fired again after another move to a new location. The first order of business was to zero in on one of the check points identified by the forward observers. This was accomplished by setting up and giving the gun crews a general compass heading. We would then fire one round at a spot we thought the FO could see. From that point on, the FO gave us add-subtract, right-left adjustments until our fire was on target. That data became the base point for all the howitzers in the location. Once we and the FO knew and assigned a name or number to the base point, he would then direct fire by moving so many yards left or right, up or down, for a new target. We always started from the base point to maintain our accuracy. It was always encouraging when the FO reported that we had nailed our targets. During the night we fired various missions to harass the enemy and keep them moving. Night missions were set up during the day to suspected hot spots identified by the FO. They were marked by name and number. The S-3 would then set up a harassment schedule and the FDC would keep track and alert the gun crews as required. If the FO wanted additional fire all he had to do was call in. We were ready at all times.

Muffled detonations all night. Flares in the sky—sputtering, phosphorescent glows that made the earth seem ethereal. I was hunched over my plotting board for hours, concentrating so hard my head ached at times. Numbing throbs pounded above my ears.

I was out in the snow again when relieved, to pace a while on the frozen ground, to limber up my legs before crawling into my bag, thanking God that I wasn't in the infantry, hunkered down face to face with the enemy. Occasionally a round would come in, exploding somewhere close by, shaking the ground, making me crawl deeper into the bag, hoping I would see morning.

On January 11 we set up in what appeared to be a factory or a mill of some kind. It was shattered, laced with bullet holes, broken machinery, papers, boxes everywhere. Snow dusted in through a massive hole in the roof. But it did have several rooms in fairly good shape. We set up the FDC in one of them. We slept in the others in case we were needed.

I heard the drone in my sleep, a far-off whine, coming closer. When I cracked my eyes I knew it was a plane, one of ours judging from the sound of its engine. It was very close. My immediate thought was that the Chinese had breached our defenses and were advancing on our position. Why else would a plane come so close? Fear took hold of me. But instead of rising, I crawled deeper into my bag. At that instant a tremendous explosion rocked the building. All the air in the room seemed to bulge. I was lifted off the floor for one intense second. The wall farthest from me shuddered, came apart, hurtled into the room in a massive burst of wood and plaster. I heard a thud above my head, as if someone had struck the wall with a sledgehammer. Dust rained down from the overhead beams. A great hush descended, broken only by those leaping to their feet.

When I looked up, all I could see was dust and smoke, and Little Joe running out of the FDC room, pulling the telephone cables with him. Someone leaped up and stopped his forward progress. Little Joe stopped, looked around. Confusion slanted across his face. His head was covered with dust. His arms were trembling. The telephone line lay tangled across his shoulder. Had he not been stopped he would have dragged the line outside, severing our communications.

I crawled out of my bag, saw what had made the noise above my head. There, less than six inches above where I lay, a large jagged piece of shrapnel was imbedded in the wall. I weakened and sagged back into the bag. Had I risen at the sound of the airplane engine, I would have taken the shrapnel right in my throat or chest. Still shaking from the experience, I burrowed down for a minute into the dark silence of my bag and thanked God for the angel on my shoulder. For me, death had taken a holiday that night. Our Air Force had laid a bomb down in the wrong grid square. Luckily no one was killed. Fortunately, I was still alive.

It was not unusual for reporters or war correspondents to make occasional stops at areas close to the front lines. I would see them occasionally, cameras slung around their necks, recorders in their hands, interviewing troops, officers, taking pictures. They were very obvious, the only ones with cameras and unending curiosities.

One day a newsman came into the factory where we had FDC set up. He wandered around for a while, took a few shots, then came up to Stallard, Little Joe and me. He introduced himself as George. I forget his last name. He was from United Press International. His handshake was firm, his smile like the side of a leaf. He wanted to know what our duties were, and where we were from. He clicked off a picture of us, looked at Stallard first.

Sefton introduced himself, said he was from New Jersey. Then Sef pointed at me, told him I was from Minnesota, that we were enlisted reserves.

He asked how long we'd been in Korea. Since December, we replied. Came over on a troop ship, were assigned to the 27th RCT. We all worked in Fire Control.

Schranck snickered, mentioned that he was in his second year of college. He was irritated that the Army had taken him. The reporter shrugged.

In an attempt to register my disdain for the call-up, I added that I had been married eight days before shipping out. That also didn't interest him.

He asked our opinion of the war. We looked at one another, grinned. I was the first to offer a frank opinion. I told him I hoped the people back home knew what we're doing here, that we'd been on the move for a month, all the way from Inchon to Kaesong, then back here, that we had the Chinese breathing down our necks. I pointed, told him the enemy was right over the hill, where we were firing.

He shrugged apathetically, indicating that he knew where they were.

I think he expected us to say something patriotic, something meaningful for the folks back home. I wasn't in the mood for answering questions, nor were Bob and Sefton. The reporter smiled, looked around. It was obvious he wanted to interview someone with more bravado. Then he looked Schranck right in the eye and asked him what he was fighting for.

I don't know what he expected to hear from Schranck, something about saving Korea perhaps, or maybe a word or two about our patriotic duty, our commitment, our willingness to stop Communism before it overwhelmed the world. Schranck didn't give him the answer he was looking for. Instead he looked right at me and, without pause, said he was fighting for his buddy.

I picked up on his comment. It was a fact. We were all fighting to save one another, to get back home. It seemed to me like an appropriate reply. I told him I was fighting for Sefton. Sefton nodded, continued the banter, said we were all fighting for one another, that we just wanted to get home.

The reporter nodded, grinned again, thanked us for our comments. I doubted that he'd use any of it in the news. It was the last we saw of George the reporter. We heard later that Paramount Pictures was over by the gun batteries taking photographs. It didn't matter to us if we were in the news. All we wanted was a ticket back home.

January 11 was another new day. It turned very cold. The snow froze like cement. All the slush and melt of a limited January thaw was now a mass of ice. Everything was frozen in. We moved into another room, away from the shattered wall, kept busy most of the morning, waited for word to move again. Hoped it would be north. We heard that our patrols had probed as far as Ich'on, east of Suwon and had met only moderate enemy resistance. Patrols to the west had made no contact. Maybe things were easing up.

We kept firing at targets north of Suwon. The radio said that General MacArthur wanted the Army to pull back to Japan. That sounded good to us. But we knew it would never happen.

7

HOLDING AREA

On January 12, 1951, the British moved in around us, forming a welcome protective blanket. On occasion I was able to talk to one of the British boys. I always came away with a high opinion of them. They were a fun bunch, upbeat, eager talkers. Although I never made any lasting friends with the British, one of the older men did tell me this was his third war. The "chap," as he wished to be called, said he had fought before World War II, had survived the terrible massacre at Dunkirk, and was now in Korea against his will.

The British had mandatory army duty starting at the age of 18, ending at 35. For their first hitch they were issued uniforms and a rifle that was theirs for the duration of their duty. The "chap" had been called up before his enlistment expired, the same as many of our own boys. It was his opinion that Harry S, as he called Truman, had done him an injustice. He felt it was America's duty to defend the world, not Great Britain's. He said we gave the Russians North Korea after the war and we now wanted the world to help us get it back for South Korea. He said at one time, "If I could ever get my hands on old Harry S, I'd choke him." Yet, for all their political disagreement and disdain for being called up by the U.N., they were a likable bunch of men.

Stallard received a canned chicken through the mail. We ate well. It was a welcome change from the "C" rations, which were becoming as tiresome as the winter.

Because I was one of the first to go forward, I was rotated back from the front position to the main body of Headquarters Battery. It wasn't a good move, because the 6 × 6 truck I was in had only a canvas cover and seats that folded up or down on each side. Those of us who went back, packed the center portion full with our gear, and tried our best to get comfortable in our sleeping bags, on the seats or on top of the gear. We were out of the wind for the most part.

The convoy stopped often, and when it did we got out to stretch. The cramped quarters and cold, drafty weather made traveling less than pleasant. The truck body was steel, about three to four feet above the ground. With the outside temperature at minus 10 degrees, the cold easily penetrated the sleeping bag, and I thought I would freeze to death. Spending the night in a truck body is excruciating. It would be better to sleep on the ground where the temperature was warmer than the air, with no wind blowing. I learned that if I could protect myself from the bottom up, I was in fairly good shape. It was a cold learning process.

Schranck had been separated from Stallard and me while we were up front in a forward FDC section. He was in a survey section. When we got back we found that he had set up a tent and saved a space so that Stallard and I would be with him in FDC. Unfortunately, two officers had seen the tent and had acquired it as their own. Schranck was livid. He told them it was our tent, which we had just moved back from forward FDC and were moving in with him.

The officers were unmoved. Rank has its privileges, they said. It was the RHIP code that was used in Korea all too often, usually at a cost to the dogface. Schranck faced up to the officers, asked them what ever happened to military courtesy. The officer tugged at his cap, told him that this was the real army, implying that the ER men just didn't understand the routine.

Schranck didn't hold back. Whenever he had something to say, he said it, whether it was to another soldier or to an officer. To his way of thinking, he was under fire and defending what was already his, reason enough to strike out despite the danger. He told the officer straight out that rank didn't mean that he had a right to treat us like puppets on a string. Then, as Stallard and I watched open-mouthed, Schranck took another step into the verbal minefield. He said the officer should be thankful that all his political desk jockeys were calling the shots, because, in civilian life, he wouldn't be able to hold down a decent job.

The end result was, the officers moved in, and we moved out.

Most of the officers considered themselves high and mighty, and our "Chief of Section" was no better. All he was interested in was the big "ME." Where his men slept was of no concern. Lesson learned.

We had a bunch of poorly educated regular army non-coms. The main officers were good men. The colonel, our CO (S-1), and Captain Joe, the operations officer (S-3), were career officers and honorable men. But the Lieutenant that was our S-2 officer was an officer who was long on time in grade but never promoted. It was the Army's way of quietly informing everyone that he was not a well-qualified officer.

The S-2 officer was involved in meetings that always took place when we moved into a new location. The top officers would meet and receive the battle orders and the targets and no-fire line information. He was responsible to bring this information to us and transfer it to our situation map that clearly designated the front line and the minimum, or no-fire, line. This was kept up to date by the map non-com, in our case, "Frenchy," a regular army man who had been there since day one. A good soldier.

The FDC was always set up in a lighted, heated situation, either a heated tent or a part of a house, but always lighted and shielded by a perimeter guard system. The section was destroyed once, and they did everything possible to assure that it wouldn't happen again. We had to be ready to receive "fire missions" or communications from headquarters 24 hours every day. I used this situation when I was on duty in the FDC to write letters to Florence and others. Some of the letters were short but many were long. I had all the current maps and situations in front of me and I used them. Mail was received and distributed at the Headquarters Battery message center where the switchboard was and where the wire crew hung out. This was the place to learn about rumors and small talk. Service Battery brought the mail daily and took back the written letters that were then relayed to the rear post office operation. Mail was a very high priority item.

We heard via the grapevine that the United Nations was about to accept Red China as a member. We hoped it would happen. Anything to shorten the war.

The command to pack up and move came almost daily. We

DICK HOLMSTEN WASHING CLOTHES. In the late spring or early summer of 1951 while our battalion was in reserve, a small spring-fed stream flowed near our unit. We formed a small dam using sandbags to provide a pool of clear, clean, cool water to wash our clothes.

always moved by truck. Packing meant getting everything into our truck and getting the truck into the convoy. The Battalion CO led the parade. Our CO (HQ Btry.) generally had planned the end location of each move. His jeep was the leader. The last truck in the HQ Btry. was the ambulance, followed by the gun batteries, all eighteen howitzers in three groups of six. Whenever the full battalion moved, Service Battery was last. The final vehicle was the large tow truck to take care of any breakdowns. A battalion move was a great event. When we moved a short distance it was generally only our HQ Battery and one or two gun batteries. One gun battery was generally in reserve. Winter conditions were just like we find them in Minnesota—cold, blowing sometimes, often wet—never very pleasant being outside like we were.

The move was only one half mile, into another village. We billeted in houses again, had the usual fire pit with two big pots over it, one for cooking, the other to keep water hot for washing. I was able to wash my fatigues and underwear. We boiled about five pair for two hours. They came out quite clean. The underwear was hung up and were dry by the next morning. With the exception of socks, I had a complete change of clothes. I planned on washing socks the following day but they came in at 01:30 and rolled us out for another alert. I found myself right in the middle of a detail assigned to pick up "C" rations. I was grabbed to ride "shotgun" on the truck. It was, in fact, a delivery service for the Wolfhound soldiers, a task we didn't complain about. We delivered 260 cases of "C-6" rations to the boys up front, enough rations for one man for six days per case or six men for one day per case.

Mail finally came through. I received letters from Florence and others. It was nice to know that I wasn't forgotten. The words of encouragement and love made me feel great. I learned that the family had a large Korean map on the wall, with pins showing approximately where I was.

So far we had traveled from Inchon to Kaesong, back to Seoul, then 20 miles south of Osan. All that time we traveled the Red Diamond highway, which was poorly blacktopped, most of it dust and dirt. Usually it was clogged with hundreds of people walking on the road and in the ditches. The army owned the road and the civilians knew it. Army trucks and MPs were at every intersection and working bridge. Regimental command controlled all convoy movements. The British were always a problem. Their rules enabled them to stop at prescribed times for tea. They would pull their convoy off the road so other trucks could go by. The British boys would all jump out, make a fire, heat water and have tea. We always poked a lot of fun at them when we came upon a stopped convoy. They always waved their teacups at us.

When the British moved, all their vehicles moved with them: the battered ones and the ones that wouldn't run. The broken ones were always towed in some fashion, because each truck was assigned to an officer. If he could not get it to a repair station, he was charged for it, so we were told. That was so different from the Americans.

When one of our vehicles became damaged, or otherwise rendered unusable, we simply pushed it off the road and burned it. No so with the Brits.

When we stopped, the boys set up a shower unit close to the riverbed. I was able to take a hot shower. It was almost the same as putting on new skin. I never thought that I'd ever see the day when one shower a month was my lot. The showers consisted of two tents placed end to end. One was used for changing. The second had a series of nozzles that sprayed hot water. There was room for about 30 men at a time. The infantry boys were the ones who really benefited.

We were FDC, a small section that usually kept to itself. We didn't conform to normal operations. We were on duty all night, slept late, ate at odd hours, answered only to the S-3 for our orders. Our chief of section was a sergeant first class, SFC, and really never warmed up to the three of us because some of the officers often gave us authority that he thought should be his.

After a frosty night, the spring day seemed brighter than it was. We were still in the village, living quite well with plenty of room and a good heating system.

To show his authority on nights without scheduled fire missions, he assigned me to walk guard duty from 06:00 to 08:00. I would walk guard again that night. At that point I got some quality sleep time. It was so hot in the shack that I had to crawl out of my sleeping bag. We were drying clothes on the floor. We didn't do much during the day. Kept clean, washed our clothes, played canasta.

Card games, smoking, stories from home—all standard. I took my ribbing as a newlywed. Honeymoon stories were common. My constant letter writing was the brunt of many jokes. The boys wondered if I had a special arrangement with the post office. I received more mail than most.

Bob Schranck told stories about growing up in Mankato, Minnesota, playing football in high school and one year at Purdue. His father had a John Deere farm implement store and was an avid hunter. Bob told of hunting pheasants in southern Minnesota and South Dakota.

Bob and I were about the same size, 200-plus pounds. Both our fathers had a family business. He had numerous girlfriends but not a steady one, unlike Florence and me before our marriage. Bob was always in trouble in the FDC operation. When he was working he was good, but sleeping made it tough for him to be on the job when we needed him. His training was more in survey. When our officers discovered that, they moved him up with the infantry as a forward observer. Bob was always fun to have around. He had more ideas on how to do bizarre things. He concocted the idea to make Welsh rabbit in a helmet. Whenever we had a quick "march order" it was always a question as to whether or not he would catch a ride. He always did but it was at the last minute. Eating was of prime importance for Bob.

Little Earl was a very small kid from New Mexico. He wasn't educated, but he was a very dedicated person. He was assigned as our 6 × 6 driver. He took excellent care of his truck. It was always gassed up and ready to go. His size was such that he had to have pillows under him and behind him to reach the pedals and to see over the steering wheel. He knew how to handle "his truck," as he called it. He was regular army. He came to Korea with the 8th Field Artillery in July of 1950. He traveled all the way with our unit. Everyone liked him.

Joe Quartararo, the kid from Philadelphia, was our radio and communications person. Little Joe had the ability to keep our telephones and radios working, whatever the situation. It wasn't his skill in radio that made him so important, rather his ability to get instant service from the radio and telephone repair section.

Sefton Stallard grew up in a well-off family. His father was president of the Elizabeth, New Jersey, Savings and Loan. He was a very active Republican, never had a good word to say about FDR or Truman. Stallard told one story about his father and friends looking forward to the election of Eisenhower. It would be a great day in the Stallard home if and when it happened. Sefton liked Scotch. His father kept him supplied by sending a bottle in a hollowed-out loaf of French bread. He was proud of that arrangement. It was the first time any of us had heard the name Sefton. Sef, as we called him, weighed all of 140 pounds, wringing wet and was about 5 feet 7 inches at most, a skinny kid, not athletic. He had attended two years at

Brown University when he was recalled in the reserve program. He never let the officers forget it. His stories about life at Brown were endless. One story was that his girl friend was joining a sorority and was in charge of a large event that required shopping for a lot of items from a department store and a supermarket. Before she arrived, he entered the store and asked to see the manager. He told the manager that his friend was a kleptomaniac, and that he would gladly pay for whatever she lifted. The manager placed a store employee as a watcher. When she was eventually stopped and questioned, she found out about the prank and hit the ceiling. We all had a good laugh at that one.

Big Joe was a big Italian kid from New Jersey. We all liked to hear his stories about life on the streets.

Stallard smoked cigarettes. Schranck, a pipe. Me, a few cigarettes just to stay awake at night. The ER men were Schranck, Stallard and Holmsten.

This was the group that usually played cards. Times of laughter. Hours of fun. A pleasant interlude to forget that war was just outside our room.

The guys in our section were great. Most were well educated. Not to imply that we were high hat, but four of us came into the outfit right out of college. We got along like brothers, worked well together in FDC. I don't know if we qualified as good soldiers, because we didn't jump for the sergeants like they thought we should. They had most of the guys under their thumbs, but not us. Renegades or not, we charted our own course. The guys in our outfit often wondered why we were never written up in the news. We read about the 1st Cavalry Division quite often. They were always in the limelight and were called "Mac's boys" by our group. When we joined the 8th FA in the north, the Chinese hit us hard. At that time, the First Cav. was east of us. They bugged out without letting our commanders know. At one point the 8th FA was the left flank of the U.S. Army. Their shoulder patch was the brunt of many jokes. It was said that the diagonal strip on the patch separated the chickenshit from the horseshit.

On January 19 we moved again to a new position, away from the valley, into the high hills, where the winds were fair. A pleasant

"HOUSEBOY," A 10–12 YEAR OLD KOREAN BOY. Somewhere along the movements we accumulated a house boy to do chores around the kitchen and the officers' tents/quarters. These locals were well treated and provided a good service for the Army.

change. The location offered Headquarters Battery better protection, higher ground, in a small cut. The snow cover was more like Minnesota, white and blinding in the sun, blue at night beneath the moon. It was there our chief of section began to discredit our group, a word here, another there, to emphasize his displeasure with our own verbal rebellion. Fortunately, Captain Joe or the CO did not support him. But he did have control over security and as such he commanded us to stand "outside guard" which meant exactly that. We were outside on our watches, not in FDC. It made me angry. He was continually on our case. We tried to ignore him as much as possible, whenever he tried to impress us with his voice. It didn't worry me. I just did my job as ordered. It was the only way to get along in the Army.

January 21—the wind was up, and it was cold in the hills, reminding me of a Minnesota day. We had a complete blackout situation, no fires allowed. Late in the afternoon they wanted all the vehicles started. Being from Minnesota, I usually had charge of the jumper cables. The boys from the South didn't understand how they worked. We were constantly fighting the cold. It was important to keep our vehicles running. I got three of the big trucks and four small trucks started, but none of the ten jeeps. When they did get started, we placed charcoal fires under the oil pans and blankets over the hoods. We started the engines every hour so they never cooled off. Had to be ready to move at a moment's notice.

When we moved into one village, a clean looking Korean kid came up and said in fair English that he was a houseboy. He was about 10–12 years old, with a gleeful grin, the type of boy who wouldn't shrug when asked a question. I took to him and he fell right in alongside wherever I went. He was a good worker. I gave him a couple of summer bags so he could sleep in our room with us. He kept the FDC clean. For this he was well fed and clothed. He was proud of his houseboy title, though he never expressed himself in English. I could tell by his swagger. He heated our wash water, kept a good fire. While we ate chow he cleaned our room and rolled out our sacks. I gave him food and smokes. He seemed very happy. He loved candy bars. No one knew where his family was, if they were dead or alive. He never expressed an opinion on anything. He just worked.

I received two boxes from home, one containing a box of Fanny Farmer candy, which Houseboy ate with gusto. Another box held cans of dates, cheese, Cheez-its, canned chicken, gum, three chocolate Christmas trees. We ate like kings. The boxes were welcome. The letters were perfect.

I was off for the entire night, listening to the constant fight between our chief of section and the first sergeant that was responsible for the headquarters battery records. It continued until Captain Joe and the CO stepped in and made them understand that, like it or not, enlisted reserve men were right for the FDC and that they handled the jobs perfectly. Listening to that banter made me much more disgusted with the Army. After the officers left, we had a rifle inspection in rank formation. The first sergeant liked to play garrison soldier. He was a real pain. We ducked him at every opportunity. Rifle inspection amounted to first getting our carbine, then proving that it was oiled and ready to fire. My God, it was always ready to fire. Our lives depended on it. We'd never disregard our weapon. We were also involved in C&C, care and cleaning of equipment. This involved just as it implied, the cleaning of all basic equipment. The radio crews accounted for theirs. The wire crews the same. Also with Medical. Garrison duty meant policing the area. Like they used to say, "Pick it up—straighten it—or paint it." The men of FDC were not immune to the characters' constant harangue.

The basics of living included slit trenches for our body waste. The latrines were dug about a foot-and-a-half wide, two-to-three feet deep. The length varied on how long we were expected to stay in one spot. Generally a tarp was put up for privacy. We entered, dropped our pants, did our thing and then covered the deposit with the dirt next to the trench. Not a very fancy way to handle things but it got the job done. If no trench was available, you simply played cat and covered up after yourself. The officers had a private arrangement that their side-boys took care of. It was definitely not the Navy way of doing things.

The food was all ration type. It came out of gallon cans inside the kitchen section, beef, gravy, powdered spuds, dehydrated carrots. The cooks made bread and we had fruit at most meals. Coffee also. Usually in the morning we had powdered eggs, hotcakes or Spam. Occasionally we had juice. We liked that. We received fresh food twice a month—a real treat.

I had three changes of wool underwear at the time, OD pants, field pants over that. On top of the summer undershirt, a long sleeved wool drawer and an OD shirt. I also had a jacket with pile lining, a pile lined cap and big leather mittens with wool inserts. On my feet, I wore one pair of light stockings and two pair of heavy socks with my shoepacks. I changed socks as often as possible and washed them by hand. "Houseboy" was a big help when it came to boiling my fatigues. I was fairly clean, with hot water enough to wash my hands and face every day, my feet occasionally. A shave every other day kept me looking trim. Time being a premium, we did what we could.

Until then I had had only two haircuts since landing in Korea. "Houseboy" was kind enough to find a village barber. He was efficient enough to hack away at my long growth. I paid him with two packs of cigarettes.

Bob Schranck came back from the front. His only comment was that they were busy, closer to the guns than they liked. Normally they were between infantry headquarters and the howitzers, which made wire connections relatively short and quick. When they were up front they were with the gun crews, a new experience, and noisy. Not the best for sleeping. After listening to him bitch, we gassed up the vehicles, a long ordeal because we had only 5-gallon cans to fill from 55-gallon barrels. We filled four trucks and two jeeps, drew some for the gas stove in the CP. Afterwards, we played canasta until dinner.

Rifle inspection happened again the following day. We were told we were getting a new first sergeant. It meant little to me, worried some others. Change was never well accepted.

In the afternoon we had a pleasant surprise. Special Services came through with a movie. It was *Ticket to Tomahawk*. It was in color and starred Dan Daily and Ann Baxter. Movies were shown either in a squad tent (room for 15 crowded) or in a room in a village house, which was not often.

We always had 110-volt power for our radios and lights in FDC. That was a perk we took advantage of from time to time. I had done a fair amount of wiring back home, so tapping a wire was not a challenge once we acquired the necessary items to make it work. On occasion I got wire, tape, and bulb outlets from the wire section, tapped into a hot 110-volt set of wires, and ran a line to our room. Once we had lights, we could do virtually anything after dark, except during periods of blackout. The energy theft was not totally appreciated by others because they felt we received special treatment. But it did elevate me to a new height of appreciation.

We left Chowan and moved halfway back to Osan, in a valley, about 15 miles off the highway. Guard duty again from 24:00 to 02:00. The temperature hovered somewhere around 10–15 degrees above zero. We were out in the weather all the time when we were not in FDC. We ate in the open. The houses were a wreck. No shelters, nothing that would allow us to get inside. Wind and snow were always with us. I don't know how "Houseboy" stood it in his two summer sleeping bags. Endurance must have been one thing all Koreans were born with.

The sweater Florence had been knitting arrived on January 24. It was one item of clothing I wore daily. It fit perfectly, looked good and was great against the cold.

Shortly after lunch, we were told to move again. At 03:00 we pulled out. It was snowing lightly. Nothing ahead of us but stark white hills, a rib of black road, and an enemy we were intent on killing.

8

RESERVE AREA

January 26, north of Osan, back in FDC. Our group rebellion against Army rules and regulations did not accomplish anything except to make the first sergeant and the computer chief fed up with our sounding off at them. It also led to the transfer of Bob Schranck to survey, Stallard to the wire section. It meant that I would be out in the cold again but back to FDC whenever there was work to do.

I was worried with Stallard in "wire." The lines were fed from the switchboard to the infantry and to the division artillery in the rear. We were wire-connected to the gun batteries on a direct line, as were the forward observers through the infantry switchboard. Wire had to be laid when we advanced and retrieved when we moved or retreated. The wire boys were a busy bunch, with a high casualty rate, because the wires were generally laid in the ditches, as were the land mines. It was never clear to me how the crews kept track of who belonged to what wire. They used ¾-ton trucks with a tripod arrangement that held the wire on rolls. The crews ran alongside the trucks as they spread the wire. They had a cranking arrangement when they retrieved the wire. The wire crews worked very hard and never received much credit. One thing to Stallard's credit: he wasn't dumb. He wouldn't make many mistakes.

I wore the sweater Florence sent me over my layers of clothes, beneath my jacket. It was a constant effort to keep clean. I'd been in my pants and shirt combination since we moved out of Seoul. Changing underwear, however, was vital. Failure to keep clean underneath would lead to a good case of KK, or Korean Krud as it was called. The only way to get rid of it was to shower, and that was a luxury rarely afforded. My feet were still in good shape. No sores.

We fired harassment missions at night. The Chinese were not

very mobile. They walked most of the time. Their advances were slow. It was an easy matter to stay ahead of them, to pin them down, to keep them awake.

Whenever Recon Company found a core of Chinese they would report it to us. They would then engage in a firefight and call upon us for artillery support. Based on the information supplied, we set up our firing schedules for harassment and future aiming points.

On January 27 we were still on the move north, between Osanni and Suwon, not on line, but close enough for me. Went through a bombed out village. Buildings were standing but all the windows and doors had been blown out. All the inside furniture was gone, taken away when the residents had fled. The thatched roofs and clay walls were the only useable parts of the structures. We had to cover the windows for blackout and wind. Makeshift stoves came out. In time it was livable. Smiley, Stallard and I moved into one shack with a fair sized room. At least we were out of the cold. Two tough, wrinkled old ladies lived in the other room of the house, not connected with ours. They had somehow lasted out both sides going through, perhaps by sheer determination and guts. We got them to help us with fires and cooking. They would do practically anything for food.

General Ridgeway rode by the next day, his jeep emblazoned with his standard. His was followed by three jeeps filled with MPs, each with their sirens blaring. Ridgeway traveled in style. The General had a brace of hand grenades strapped across his jacket, and a polished pistol at his waist. I heard him say "good morning" as he passed me. He looked like a man who could get things done. The mere sight of him evoked a feeling of determination and resolve. Rules stated that, even in combat, you saluted the flag of a general. In our outfit saluting was not done. None of the officers had their rank showing. It made them too much of a mark. We did, however, salute Ridgeway.

We woke up to a beautiful day, bright sun, melting snow, our first nice weather in a long time. I wrote a letter outside, with a pencil, using a board as my desk. The ball in my pen was stuck. Despite the warm weather, I acquired a cold and had to see the medic to get some cough syrup.

I received a box from home containing ski socks, which came

up over the knees, a rough wool weave, perfect for the Korean weather. Nothing fancy, but practical.

Had guard duty from 02:00 to 04:00 with a bit of excitement. The Chinese tried to slip into our area. The infantry units and guards located them while I was on duty in FDC. A firefight occurred not far from our location. I heard a round coming in, ran toward the trucks, tripped over a trailer tongue, sprawled flat in the snow. One clumsy soldier. The outside guard for the FDC was put on extra alert. When my shift changed, I went to bed.

The following day the boys in one of our gun batteries brought in a couple of Chinese prisoners. They were a poorly dressed lot, in canvas shoes, tattered uniforms, a roll of rice that extended like a horseshoe over their shoulders. They were given a roll of rice when they left on a campaign. The quantity of rice remaining in the roll indicated how long they had been in the field. All they needed was boiling water and they had a meal. The pair I saw were sorry excuses for soldiers. Their rice rolls were nearly empty. Our officers tried to get something out of them, but couldn't. They were taken to the POW camp and were found to be Chinese Nationals. I never found out what happened to them.

The Suwon airstrip was just to our left. It operated daily, with Mustangs, spotter planes and freighters coming and going all the time. Late in the afternoon General MacArthur's four motor *Constellation* and six fighters came in, which created quite a stir.

The following morning, when Stallard, Schranck and I were playing canasta in our room, the first sergeant came in. He paused at the door only long enough to tell us there were more important things to do than playing cards. He said we had to unload a squad tent and put it up.

I slammed down my cards, told him we had late watch, that we weren't on duty. There were other sandbaggers who could do the work. He glared at me, told me it was an order. He should have known better, not to get a Swede mad. I told him to get lost.

He took a John Wayne stance, hand on hips, and asked me to repeat what I'd said. Again, I told him to get lost. His face reddened. He called me an insubordinate son-of-a-bitch. I agreed, then told him to find someone else to carry his tent.

Angered to the point of incineration, he threatened to go to CP. The command post was where the battery commander and the other brass were. His only hope was to disgrace us as troublemakers.

As he walked out the door, I stood up and followed him. I thought it best that the commander hear my own words, not his. We walked fast, he ahead of me by ten paces. When we got there he told them about my disobeying an order.

I explained in a voice somewhere between calm and anger that our group had been up all night on watch. There were a dozen other men just laying around doing nothing. I also explained that the first sergeant had opposed us ever since we arrived, because we were ER, and that he knew the rules as well as we did. We were off duty. Off duty means we had private time. On duty meant we worked. There were others on duty who could lug his tent.

The commander chewed on his cigar and in regulatory fashion asked the first sergeant if we were off duty. He said we were but added that we were playing cards when there was work to be done.

The commander turned to me, looking for a tactful ruling that would satisfy both parties. He asked us to pitch in for the sergeant, provided that he helped with the work. We were to unload the tent, and the sergeant and the rest of the section would put the thing up while we played cards. That way we wouldn't disobey an order. It sounded fair.

The commander had a soft spot in his heart for the enlisted reserve. He realized the price we had paid for leaving our families on a moment's notice, and it appeared as though he understood the manner in which the sergeant treated us, with disrespect. Anyway, we unloaded the tent and were very content to watch the sergeant and the others put it up. We returned to the card game with our pride intact.

Moved again on January 31. We left the airstrip about 10:00 and set up again somewhere northeast of Suwon but not in a town. Our setup was in CP, in the big tent. No houses that time. We were dug in next to a large earthen bank. My bag was under a straw roof with no sides.

The move placed us within Chinese mortar range. After taking a few rounds from them, we got help from the 155mm howitzers to quiet them down. We fired about 120 rounds on my shift as requested by the forward observers, more after that. It was a fitful night's sleep. The 155s kept pounding away.

The generator quit somewhere toward morning. I was rustled out, told to get it going. Finally got the thing started. At 08:00 we started firing again, kept it up most of the day.

Schranck was out as FO. He was on the top of a ridge when his jeep started to get away from him. He jumped to safety but the jeep careened down the hill and ended up a pile of wreckage. One less vehicle in the outfit. Bob wasn't hurt. He got back safely.

The Turkish infantry moved in around us. I had very little contact with them. It was rare that they came into our compound. When they did, they always brought an interpreter along. One thing was certain: the Turks were a wild group. Fighting fools.

9

SUPPORTING THE TURKS

By January 10 I was in a small group of Headquarters Battery, FDC Division, on special liaison work, to form a tighter link between our division, our battalion and the infantry, and to strengthen overall plans for artillery support. Our role at Division artillery had changed from merely directing artillery fire, to that of planning future harassment missions and to coordinate overall artillery fire with other units. We learned about time on target (TOT), a procedure where Division was responsible for coordinating massive artillery fire from different units to land on a prearranged target at the same time. The next step was to get a number of different battalions involved. At certain times this procedure went all the way to the offshore Navy. The official TOT clock was set at 60 minutes to countdown, during which time all units would set their own fire missions, designed so their rounds would land on the target at exactly the same time. That way, the big boys could fire their rounds ahead of ours, so that all the fire came down like rain from hell. I witnessed a TOT strike soon afterwards. It was devastating. If anything survived that concentrated fire it was only by the grace of God. I had never seen anything so destructive.

All this was done at a time when we were trying to outguess the Chinese. They did with pure numbers what we did with machines and power. I hate to think how many of them died while trying to reach their objectives. War, I thought, was such a waste of human life. Who in their right mind would choose it in preference to peace? I will never be able to answer that question. Perhaps the only way to stop it would be to put the politicians on the battlefield.

It snowed hard, wet and heavy flakes the size of a dime. The temperature hovered somewhere in the teens. Mud everywhere. The trucks were mired up to their axles. It seemed as if the rice paddies had no bottoms. Several of our howitzers bogged down; we had to get one of the heavy-duty tow trucks to yank them out. Even when the paddies froze, the ice was thin, easy to break through. Mud oozed out like black sludge.

I didn't carry much on that trip because I knew we would move often, and fast. We had six men to the ¾-ton truck, our bedrolls, FDC equipment and our "C" rations. We had been restocked so our food supply was good. We had pork and beans, spaghetti, vegetable soup and pork patties, all packed in preservatives. One can per meal, along with a second can of hard biscuit with jelly, cocoa powder or coffee powder. Actually, the biscuits were thick crackers that held up to a jelly spread. We opened the cans with a small can opener carried on the same chain as our dog tags. It also served as a screwdriver when needed. We generally ate the main course hot, but not without effort. If possible, we would heat the can in one of two ways. The best way was to find a container that would hold enough water so the can could be completely covered and heated to boiling. When it boiled we would take the can out and open it as soon as possible and eat the heated main course. We heated the water on open fires. Some men had small heaters or camp stoves. Heating was not always possible, but you soon figured out ingenious ways to obtain heat. Sometimes we used our helmets as the water container. This was risky because the helmet wasn't deep enough to cover the can completely. Water for cooking was often scarce. Drinking water was not always easy to find when we were on rations. Water was treasured. Whatever was left went for cooking.

"C" rations provided 3,800 calories daily in battle conditions, when it wasn't possible to set up a mess hall. We were supposed to dispose of the empty cans in common pit, but that didn't happen often. We were typical GIs. We pitched them, as careless soldiers did when on the run. The men in our group were fortunate. We had a wonderful food chain from home and we guarded the horde greedily among ourselves. Sharing within the group was standard. Those outside the group could fend for themselves.

I had a bag with three extra socks, a shaving kit, insoles for my boots and my winter, down-filled bedroll, waterproofed with my shelter half. When I slept outside I just rolled it out and crawled in, dirty clothes and all. My boots were kept right next to me, except for the insoles, which were taken into the bag with my clothing. Being dirty was something I tolerated. Showers were taken between moves, when the timing was right.

I was being called out for fire missions on a regular basis. Free time became shorter and shorter, as scarce as tulips in January. On February 1, we fired 1,300 rounds, then found out that we would get only 250 rounds per battalion per day because of a supply foul-up. Not good news, especially when the forward observers were calling in new targets on an hourly basis. The limit of 250 rounds meant that we could fire only 80 rounds per battery, per day.

Our captain, the officer in charge, had been in the artillery during World War II. He was not above going around the rules when the need arose. He figured that 250 rounds weren't adequate to meet our needs. So he took a couple of empty trucks back to the ammunition supply point. When he came back he had not only our ration, but the ration for the 1st Cavalry Division artillery, which included three artillery battalions. How he did this was anyone's guess. It was rumored that he signed off as a 1st Cavalry officer and that the sergeant in charge accepted his signature as genuine and loaded the trucks.

The next day all hell broke loose in our FDC. We were questioned by the brass, but of course we knew nothing about the extra ammunition we had received. Dumb soldiers right to the end. Lots of shoulder shrugging, and hidden laughter. The captain sweated for a day or two before the incident blew over. We never had any compassion for the 1st Cavalry. As far as we were concerned they belonged to MacArthur, existed mostly for show and could get whatever they wanted just by waving a finger. The longer I was in the war, the more I realized it was dog eat dog, survival of the fittest, even behind the lines where gold braid was law.

By this time our position in the 8th Field Artillery was in direct support of the Turkish Infantry Regiment, much the same as we supported the 27th Regiment. Although our group seldom came in direct contact with the Turks, we did, on occasion, stray into their territory. On one occasion I recall we were close to their command post on a day when they brought in a group of Chinese prisoners. Their way of handling them was quite different from ours. While we would conscientiously interrogate them and eventually truck them away to a POW camp, the Turks had a more barbaric way of treating them. They would form a circle around the Chinese and bat them around inside the circle until they couldn't stand. Then they would drag them away. It was both punishment and entertainment, we supposed. The day I observed the punishment, I stood nearby under the glare of disapproving eyes, watching, my arms at my sides. They tried to wave me away, but I didn't move. I stood silently while listening to the sounds of their fists, the cries of the prisoner, the laughter from the circle of huge men who seemed specifically selected for the job. Eventually one of our officers stepped in and insisted that the treatment be stopped. The Turks were not happy with the interference. They complained that we had no business messing in their affairs. But they did stop. I think we saved a few Chinese from being severely beaten or possibly killed. The Turks were a brutal bunch of men. They didn't like the war any more than we did, and they expressed themselves in an extremely hostile manner, especially with prisoners.

On January 12, Smiley, our computer man, Willie, the intelligence sergeant, and I took time out from our normal duties and hiked to the top of a nearby hill to watch an air strike that was already underway. From the hill we could see the Chinese activity with field glasses. They were about two or three miles distant, across the valley, holed up in the hills. The infantry had apparently called in the strike to flush them out. The planes, P-51s, came in very low and dropped cans of napalm on the hills that had already been worked over by artillery. Nothing was there but gouged earth, shattered trees, battlefield refuse, the dead. The pilots were amazing fliers, with pinpoint accuracy. Some of them dropped their cans right into caves, covering everything with an enveloping balloon of flame that incinerated everything in a gush of fire. Even at our distance, I swore we could feel the heat. We were stunned by the show. It was the first time I had seen a napalm attack. All Smiley could say when a canister exploded was, "Holy shit." But despite our exuberance, the situation turned serious in seconds.

It all happened so fast, I hardly had time to catch my breath. A P-51 came over directly above us, headed for the hillside. The plane had no sooner cleared our hill than I saw sections of its fuselage peel away in a puff of black smoke. The aircraft slanted left, twisted and in the flash of an eye, the pilot ejected. He came out, a tumbling black ball, as the plane nose-dived into the ground. His chute opened almost immediately. I watched as he came down in the valley, somewhere between us and the Chinese. I didn't waste any time. I wheeled, tore down the hillside and headed toward FDC. Smiley and Willie stayed behind to pinpoint the spot where the pilot had landed.

I tore into FDC, immediately saw the major. I ran up to him breathlessly, told him one of our planes went down, that we saw the pilot's chute open a mile from the Chinese lines.

The major wasted no time. He asked how many men were up on the hill with me. I told him two, Smiley and Willie. He said we needed three more, one driver and two medics, that I was to take the ¾-ton truck. He would get the medics. As an afterthought, he made sure I had my carbine. As we parted, I heard him say he was calling in a chopper.

I ran to the truck, rousted Little Joe out of a catnap. Together we waited as two medics came running. The four of us tore off for the top of the hill. When we got there, Smiley was pointing frantically, down near the shell craters. The pilot's chute was there, spread out like a huge fan.

One of the medical officers took charge. We were to stay put, to cover them while they went down on foot. The medics started down the steep, ragged incline. The going was slow. We could see that the pilot had started making his way toward us. It appeared he was limping. Probably wounded.

Before the medics reached the bottom of the hill, we heard the chopper coming from behind. As he came over, we engaged his frequency on our radio and directed him accordingly. It took him only a moment to respond.

We worked our way over to a ridgeline where we could see them clearly. Nothing but mud there. Black pudding we called it. But it was a good vantage point, with a clear line of sight. If any Chinese came near them we could pick them off. At that point we were between the infantry lines and the Chinese. Not a good place to be. It didn't occur to us that we were in trouble. Luckily we didn't receive any fire from the opposite hills. The napalm must have made them dig deeper. I think they were afraid to come out. We stayed low and crawled our way out of the mud. We didn't want to attract attention.

When the helicopter lifted off, the medics went with them. We turned tail then and drove the jeep back to FDC. By the time we returned chow was over. But they had saved some for us. Heroes for the moment. It felt good, to have done something positive for a change, to have saved a life. It was a pleasant alternative to killing.

Later, I opened my mail. Some of it was late from Fort Lawton: fruit cake, cookies, other goodies intended for Christmas. But they were still in good shape.

February 3: Day firing was easier for the gun batteries than night firing. The gunner for each howitzer had his eyepiece focused on the aiming stake. When the command came down to adjust fire to the left or right, by degrees, all he had to do was move his scale accordingly. This was called deflection correction. It started at the HCO table as instructed by the forward observer.

The next responsibility for the gunner was the vertical adjustment, a setting received from the VCO operator. This came in the form of a degree setting, justified by a change in distance, after the HCO operator and the VCO operator had applied the corrections. The charge setting, type of charge, and number of rounds for effect had all been set when the fire mission was first established. After firing the mission, the gun would again be focused on the aiming stake.

At night the gunners put a light on the aiming stake, because focusing was much harder. For the most part blackout was maintained. It was also more difficult to see the scales on the gun.

The gun crews' shelters were a conglomeration of just about anything that could be scrounged, wood, ammunition boxes, sandbags, parts of buildings, barrels, cans, anything solid enough to create walls. The gun crews were very ingenious people who made living quarters out of discards, anything to improve the holes in which they lived.

When a fire mission was announced, it was an immediate call to action. All hands dropped whatever they were doing and took up their prescribed locations. This could be a location to unbox and prepare ammunition as soon as the type and charge was announced or at the gun itself. If the mission was an unexpectedly large one, they often roused the officers and other enlisted men not on duty. But they knew they had better have a damn good reason to roust out the brass.

A "chart mission" was another way of describing a prearranged mission. The forward observer would pick out potential trouble spots and we would fire one gun, adjust on that target, and name or number it for future reference. In this way, if the FO saw trouble all he had to do was call for support fire on target by number and name, knowing that all the adjusting had already been done. This was particularly effective if he wanted harassment fire at night.

Our FO had been assigned on temporary duty, as part of the Turkish Infantry Regiment, to work with a company interpreter, so he could tell us in English what the Turk officers were requesting in their language.

One morning we were in direct close support and had a coordinated planned attack time. It was a very foggy morning. We were told to hold fire and stand at the ready, to fire at a moment's notice as soon as the fog lifted. They would attack as we fired, to keep the Chinese pinned down in their trenches and holes.

The delay went on for longer than expected. When the fog lifted suddenly, as if swept away by a hand, we heard a terrible commotion from the infantry area but no request for fire. When we finally did get the FO on the phone, he told us that as the fog lifted, the Turks realized the Chinese had moved forward. There was no room for an artillery barrage. The battle, once engaged, was hand-to-hand combat. The Turks lost men, but not nearly as many as the Chinese. When the Chinese finally fell back we fired to keep them retreating.

After the battle, the engineers brought a shower unit close to our location and we shared hot water with the Turks. Nothing was better than a hot shower after living and fighting all winter in the same clothes. We appreciated the Quartermaster Corps when new clothes came through. Before showering, our dirty clothes went in a pile to be burned. We kept our boots and wallets protected, then went into the shower which was nothing more than a large tent with a wooden sectional floor and a ring of shower heads all being fed by a large heater that drew water from a nearby stream, or from a water truck, whichever was available. The GIs thought this was great, but the Turks had a problem.

The Turkish culture did not permit them to stand naked in a group. We, or course, could not understand this and watched the show with interest. They did not take off their T-shirts or shorts when entering the shower. Instead, in order to get clean, they would pull their shorts and shirts away from their bodies and wash their body parts underneath them, thus maintaining their dignity. This made for a lot of conversation, but no smart remarks by anyone. The last thing we wanted near us was an angry Turk.

February 5: I wrote a letter on watch, alone with my thoughts and my memories. Quiet time, the best time, hoping the FO wouldn't call. Went to the sack at 03:15. Was up again at 05:00 to the sound of commotion.

It wasn't mission fire, but rather a house fire that caused the ruckus. We had been staying in a local house that had a good thatched roof. The Papa-san had stayed in the house as a way of protecting his property. We had rigged up a stove with a chimney through the roof, rather than using the conventional, under-the-floor system that was normal for the locals. We didn't realize that the chimney would get hot enough to start the thatched roof on fire. But it did. When I dashed outside, the roof was ablaze, and everyone was making a mad dash to find water.

The Papa-san didn't panic. He knew well enough that the GIs would try to pour water on the fire. He also knew it wouldn't work. The fire in a thatched roof starts at the bottom and works its way up. He knew the only way to save the house was to pull the roof off. That is what he did. With the help of the GIs, he pulled down the burning part and stomped it out on the ground, leaving the rest of the roof untouched. His calm and deliberate action meant that we wouldn't have to move. Finding another place as good as the one we had would have been impossible. We were lucky to have had the

Papa-san there when he was needed. His rewards were many. And, he had saved his house.

On occasion, Bob Schranck and I talked to the warrant officer about putting in a request to attend OCS, Officers Candidate School. We knew it was located in Fort Riley, Kansas. If selected, it would mean a trip out of Korea and back to the States. We had no idea how long the war would last. As far as we knew, the Chinese had millions of men they could put into the field. The war could last for years, perhaps decades. OCS seemed a likely way out. The only hitch was, the government wanted three additional years of active duty from us at the conclusion of the school. But we were dreamers. We thought perhaps if we did get accepted, and graduated, the army would have far too many officers on its hands and we would be dropped. Desperation was our guiding influence. I wanted desperately to get back to Florence. Schranck had his own agenda.

Our discussions didn't go very far, but they did keep our hopes alive. In preparation for possible reassignment, I wrote Florence for a copy of my birth certificate, my high school diploma and my university transcript with grades. Those forms had to accompany the OCS application, which would take about two months to clear. The whole idea was to get back home. Stallard said we were "whistling Dixie," which was another way of saying we didn't have a chance. I believed the warrant officer knew we were fighting a losing battle, but he encouraged us just the same, to keep our morale up, to keep us alert. Hope was a genuine way to keep a soldier on his toes.

The Turks really caught it after dark, with mortar fire and small arms. The Chinese used the cover of darkness to attack with bugles blowing, yelling, screaming, anything to make noise. Our FO didn't dare fire into darkness unless we had charted points. Occasionally we would throw up a flare round, timed to explode high in the air with a bright phosphorous light on the end of a parachute. The 105 flares were not nearly as effective as the 155 Long Toms, but they would light up the countryside well enough for the FO to see. The mortar fire quieted down after a while. After that it was a calm night.

I received bad news from home. Bill, a distant relative and a Marine reservist, who was involved in the initial landing at Inchon, had been killed in action. My parents asked me to find out the details of his death, but that was impossible. My only intent was to inform them, and Florence, that I was safe and not to worry. It was the same war, in the same country, but Bill's mission had been different than mine. His was assault. Mine was support. The very fact that I was positioned behind the lines made for peace of mind, both in Korea and at home. Still, news of his death was unsettling.

On occasions we were harassed by a mortar round. "A" battery took a few. But nothing near FDC.

I pulled the graveyard shift. Aside from lack of sleep, it gave me a good opportunity to talk aloud, as if Florence were sitting beside me. It was a diversion for me, pretending she was there. Of course, I did all the talking. Got up at 22:00. Back to the sack at 02:30. Up again at 07:00, ate chow, cleaned up. Then we got our marching orders.

We broke down the tent, assembled the FDC equipment and prepared to move. Pulled out at 15:30, went about nine miles straight south of Young-Dong-Po. The village was small, but must have been very active prior to the war. An army camp there was being used as a replacement depot. The houses and business establishments had all been destroyed. Only shells of buildings could be seen. We ended up in a shattered house with floor heat. No sign of glass, no windows, no doors. But a building, despite its condition, was much better than a tent. Moyer made a fire under the floor. It got so hot that night I couldn't sleep. I woke up sweating, opened my bag for fresh air. Wondered what the hell I was doing there. Felt genuine anger for the first time in weeks. It was one of those agonizing moments when everything troubling seemed to come in on you, like a mortar round. How easy it would have been to cry. But that was something one didn't do. Stuffing it was always the best choice.

We hadn't been able to clip onto the lines and so the FDC room was cold when I went on duty. The stove was not working. It had backed up and filled our working area with fumes, so it was shut down. We did have lights, but worked with our breath showing. A perimeter guard had been stationed around FDC. We were a prime target. We had the situation maps and firing targets all set. We had to know where all the officers were sleeping in case we needed them. Our job was to be ready for any situation. The infantry liaison officer checked in on a regular basis. His message had to be logged. I was not a fighting soldier, but I did my job, hoping the infantry and the security guards would keep me safe and sound.

The temperature was getting chilly without heat. I tried to think of others who were sleeping out in the snow with the Chinese breathing down their necks. Whenever it got cold and miserable, I always thought of the infantry. Anything was good compared to what they had to endure.

The mail came through. I received socks, razor blades, shaving cream, laces, insoles, and the *Minnesota Daily* telling that Wes Fesler had been hired as the new head coach for football. The letter was dated February 1. Not bad. A ten-day delivery. The laces were welcomed. I had many knots in the ones that currently tied my shoes.

We moved every day. Found ourselves within range of Young-Dong-Po and were set up in what was left of a good-sized village. We had to repair a house to make it livable. The windows and doors were gone, so we found wood and boarded it up, blacked it out. We found a door for one end, a blanket for the other. Still the wind got in. There were a few holes in the walls. Stallard and I had a cubbyhole. The three radio operators had a small room to themselves, as did Schranck and John. The temperature was not that cold but the wind was raw. The sweater was my constant companion. I wore it all the time. It was my fourth layer: two undershirts (wool and summer); a wool high neck sweater; my sweater from home; a wool shirt; and my pile jacket. So damn many clothes on I could hardly move. But it was necessary.

North of us, the Allied troops had recaptured Young-Dong-Po, the Kimpo Airfield and the Inchon Airport. A South Korean patrol had probed into Seoul along with elements of the 25th Division. Troops of the 25th Recon Company, along with light tanks, entered Inchon shortly after a barrage from the big guns of the U.S.S. *Missouri* that were monitored through our FDC. The enemy perimeter in the west had collapsed, mainly from the bombardment it had taken. With the Chinese on the run again, toward the Han, we breathed a sigh of relief. The war had suddenly taken on a new dimension and the Allied forces were, once again, in charge.

I spent most of my time as HCO on the position table. We were shifting and rotating jobs among ourselves. I was then doing more VCO or vertical control operator work. That involved taking the change of distance in yards, as received from the HCO, and converting that command to degrees of elevation. My shift to chief of section did not sit well with some of the regular army men because I was being promoted in job status without being promoted in rank. In short, both Schranck and I understood the situation and didn't have a problem with it.

We got an air observer to help with targeting. The plane was an L-19, high wing Cessna, single-engine, two-place aircraft. The observer would fly low and slow and would observe the enemy from overhead. He would compare his observations with the ground observer and radio back to us with coordinates for a fire mission. His firing procedure was different than the ground FO because he would not give us a compass reading to the target, as did the FO. He could see our guns and knew where they were in relationship to his target and would give his adjustments as if he were standing behind the guns. He would say left, right, adds, subtracts, by yards, and we would accommodate him on a line of fire status. He had to be careful not to be in the line of fire because our rounds had a high trajectory. His landing strip was any straight road. He did land close to us on several occasions, just to see who he was talking to. His base of operations was the Suwon airstrip.

Trouble came later, in the form of a woman. It was mid-morning when our radio operator, Little Joe, dashed into FDC bearing an unusual message: The general was coming, and he was bringing a correspondent with him, a woman, to interview some of the ERs. It appeared that she wanted to write about us. The major wanted me and Stallard to come over to the tent.

Neither Sef nor I wanted to go. I knew what she wanted to hear, that we were brave men fighting against Communism on a foreign shore. Standard tripe. Nothing of the real situation.

Little Joe was impatient. Stallard said he'd go. I finally agreed, told him to do the talking. He was the one with the silver tongue. He said his speaking skill was loquacious.

We left the house, walked toward the tent where the lady was waiting. The general's jeep was parked outside. It seemed Little Joe had been telling the truth. Bob and I stared at one another, shrugged, mentally prepared our stories. We entered the tent. The general wasn't there, but the major was. Beside him stood a woman and a photographer. The cameraman snapped a picture. The major nodded his approval and stepped forward, introduced us to Miss Beatrice, from the *New York Times*, said she had came up from Suwon to interview some of the men in FDC. She wanted to do a story on the enlisted reserves' part in this war.

Miss Beatrice was a blonde. Her hair was brushed up and snuggled beneath a combat helmet. Her eyes had the look of an inquisitor, sharp, piercing, straight ahead contact. She was a slender woman. Her figure was hidden behind layers of clothing, combat fatigues being her outer garment. She wore no makeup. There was a smudge on her cheek that she hadn't bothered to wipe away. It gave her credibility. She said she was here on behalf of her newspaper, trying to get a first hand impression of the war. She was particularly interested in the role the enlisted reserves were playing, and what our morale was at this point of the struggle. She asked if we would answer a few questions.

We introduced ourselves as she jotted notes on a pad. As she wrote, the major explained that we played a very important role in fire direction. He emphasized the fact that we were all well educated college boys, which is why we held down critical positions. Then he left it up to us to give her the full story.

As the major left the tent, the photographer moved to a position behind Miss Beatrice. She looked around uneasily as if the tent were confining. Then she frowned, said it was too dark inside. She wanted to move outdoors, in the sunlight.

We walked outside and went to where the jeep was parked. She sat down in the driver's seat while we stood alongside the vehicle. The wind cut across her face. She shielded herself behind the glass. Her smile was forced. She appeared tired, perhaps from the drive up from Suwon. She asked how long we'd been in Korea.

Stallard explained that we all came together, on the same troop ship out of Seattle.

She noticed the wedding ring on my finger, asked if I was married. I told her I was, just before I left the States. She replied that she was also married, that she preferred to be with her husband and not interviewing soldiers in Korea. I guess she thought that made us equals in a way. She twisted in her seat and smiled briefly before continuing her questioning. She wanted to know about us, where we came from, what we did. One by one, we obliged.

Stallard squared his shoulders, told her he was in college, majoring in finance, when Uncle Sam came knocking at his door. He had his future all planned, had a real opportunity awaiting him after graduation with the Elizabeth Savings and Loan, his father's business. Now, he grumbled, he was shooting at the Chinese.

I was next. I told her I was a college boy, just like Stallard. I joined the Army for a one-year hitch starting in September of 1948 so that I would complete my military requirements and return to the University of Minnesota football program without losing a year of eligibility. This one-year plan required that I join the reserves. This was a good plan until June 25, 1950, when this Korean conflict started. I was working for my father in 1950, when Truman sent me a letter saying I had to report for active duty. My father owned a commercial refrigeration business in St. Paul.

Schranck had more gripes than both Stallard and I. He explained that he had been pulled out of school just as his Dad was preparing to put him to work at his John Deere implement business in North Mankato. He went on to explain how disillusioned he was. In fact, he said, he was downright pissed. He had had the world by the tail before Old Harry decided he needed some fresh meat to fight the war in Korea.

She wrote as she talked, telling us that Old Harry didn't have much to do with it. It was the North Koreans who decided to invade the South. Old Harry had merely responded to the Communist threat. She looked critically at us, brushed her hand across her mouth, looked down at her paper. Slowly, she shook her head, an obvious indication of her displeasure.

Stallard didn't wait for her to ask another question. He jumped right in, telling her we joined our outfit when they were north of the 38th parallel around the first week of December, how they gave us summer sleeping bags. Summer bags! Obviously the politicians had thought this fracas would be over by Christmas. Why else would they issue sleeping bags that wouldn't last through the first frost? Of course they never told the Chinese we had summer sleeping bags. Maybe if they had, they would have stopped fighting. As it was, they came down, drove us out of Seoul, pushed us as far south as Suwon, testing our artillery all the way. Finally, by God, we stopped them and were now pushing north again, to get more men across the border. Back and forth. Back and forth. Killing for killing. He said it didn't seem like we were gaining anything but graves. First the NK blasted across the 38th parallel and pushed the civilians out of their country. Then we got the United Nations involved and they sent over a couple of understaffed divisions to Pusan where they almost got annihilated. Then the ROKs got involved and more U.S. troops were sent over, along with the Marines. Then we pushed them all the way back to the Yalu and would have beaten them had not the politicians allowed the Chinese to mass thousands of troops in complete safety on their side of the river. They thumbed their noses at us, they did. Finally when the weather was cold and we were not equipped with winter gear, they blew their damned bugles and poured across the Yalu like ants, and started the war all over again. The Marines caught hell. This Division was lucky. We were split in two and forced down the Red Dog Highway. Others were forced East. You know the sad story. It was like they wanted them to come and get us.

She said he sounded cynical.

He agreed. He didn't have one good thing to say about how the war was being fought.

Her eyes moved to Schranck, silently prodding him.

He was direct, said we had more and better troops now, but that there was talk about not letting us finish what the North Koreans had started, even though we got our asses kicked. Now the top brass was saying that we had to hold them to the 38th parallel.

She talked some more, tried to get us shifted to a different point of view. We weren't receptive. The cameraman took a few more shots, then laid his camera down in the jeep, waited for her to conclude the interview. By this time she was totally unimpressed with us, with our stories and with our attitudes. We could tell by her facial expressions that she had wasted her time. She wanted to hear that our morale was high and that we were fighting to put down aggression and Communism. Our collective opinion was that it would never be done with arms and men and we made that clear to her.

Finally she said we hadn't given her anything, that we were merely three disgruntled GIs who would rather close their eyes to the real problem than face up to it.

I asked her what the real problem was. She said she was going to find some other soldiers to give her the right answer. That was all right with us. I, for one, wanted out of the questioning.

She slid her pen into her pocket. In conclusion, she asked us if we were soldiers who had taken an oath to protect our country against its enemies and why were we so all-fired angry to be fulfilling that pledge.

I was a bit irritated by now. Her question bordered on the inflammatory. I told her simply that Korea was not our country. I was ready to turn away when she said that the North Korean invasion was a threat to our government and our way of life.

I gritted my teeth, tried to cool my rising anger. I said if that was true, then we should be allowed to finish the job. We needed to push these Chinese back where they belonged instead of playing a continual game of cat and mouse.

She sighed, agreed with what I had said, put on a new and delightful smile, then looked toward the mess tent. She said she was hungry, wanted us to take her through the chow line so she could rough it with the guys.

We went to the mess tent. I was the one to find her a mess kit and a fork, minus the spoon and cup. She was not impressed when I rinsed the mess kit in the boiling water and then handed it to her. As she reached for it, it fell into the dirt at her feet. Indignantly, she picked it up and laid it on the table. A cook came to her rescue. He found an officer's plate, cup and tableware and gave them to her. As she sat down with us to eat, I was sure she wanted to be elsewhere.

Stallard continued to talk during the meal. He continued to tell her what a raw deal we had received and how we had traveled up and down on the peninsula like a yo-yo. She hadn't expected this kind of response from us and after a rushed meal she leaned over and said we were nothing more than "pseudo intellects." Disappointed in us, she said she was going to find someone who could give her a better insight as to what we were doing over here. As far as she was concerned, we could go back to our sacks.

She left us and found the public information officer. He took her around and found her a man named Dan. He was Regular Army and had been in for three years. During that time he had a rough time making PFC as a driver. He was not very bright. But she heard exactly what she wanted to hear. Dan filled her with the rah-rah glory stuff and what a good job we were doing to defeat Communism. She took it all down, took his picture several times over, once by a ¾-ton truck. He took a gas can and faked pouring it, into the radiator of all places. We stood nearby and hooted. She proceeded to interview other "muscle heads" who thought our morale was at 100 percent. She wrote down only what she wanted to hear. I'm sure our stories went in the fire. It was my opinion that Miss Beatrice left with a very poor opinion of reservists, despite the fact that we were fighting the war exactly as we were trained to do, exactly as we had pledged. As far as I was concerned, duty had very little to do with opinion.

As she was about to leave she requested the use of a latrine. Being the closest to her, I pointed to an officer's tent. She thought it was the latrine. The other guys with me couldn't believe their eyes when she entered the tent. A short time later she came out and went on her way.

We were not surprised when the officer finally returned to his tent only to find her waste and her dirtied paper in plain sight. He demanded to know who directed her into his tent. Of course, no one knew. To this day, I have no idea if Miss Beatrice's article was ever printed in the *New York Times*.

I wondered if the reporters had ever seen anyone hit by white phosphorous, a jelly gas bomb or a land mine? They hadn't had to worry about an incoming round. I wished they would tell the public how costly this war was in good American lives, that China has fought for 2,000 years and could continue to fight for another 2,000. Where did this put us? As we became weak from the loss of American lives, we waited for the Russians to step in. All I wanted was to be home with my wife, to live a life together like we started after our wedding.

I went to my sack that night a bit more disillusioned than in the morning. The whole thing about searching for a story, and finding only the reaction they desired, put my appreciation for news reporters at the bottom of my list, right next to lawyers and politicians.

We moved again and were now in direct support of the ROK infantry. We were about 6,000 meters from Seoul or about one-half mile. The Chinese didn't give up the ground easily. They resisted ferociously, sacrificing men as if they had an inexhaustible supply. We prepared for an all-out attack, to break their back, to stop us from making another costly retreat. Yet, they said if we went north, beyond the 38th parallel, it would be a political headache. No one knew what was up. We had to man FDC 24 hours every day, and be ready for instantaneous fire missions. We made frequent "commo checks," communications checks, to make sure all our stations were on line and ready.

We were in a valley, living in a dilapidated farmhouse. The temperature was comfortable for a change. The battery put up the big squad tent and showed a movie, *Milkman*, with Jimmy Durante. It was a poor picture, but it killed some time.

Firing. Firing. Firing. Constantly. It seemed doubtful that I would ever get a good night's sleep again.

Dog tired, worn out, sleep deprived, exhausted. It was a soldier's punishment.

10

ROUTINES

On the evening of February 13, I had my first night off in three weeks. Slept like a babe. Huddled deep in my bag, I didn't hear the firing that went on until 20:00. Stallard awoke me for chow. He told me that an infantry outfit had found a bag of mail alongside the road. When they looked into it they found that it belonged to the Headquarters Battery of the 8th FA, our outfit. It had been ransacked. All the packages were gone. Only letters remained, none of which were mine. The brass informed us to tell our people back home that they might get some phony mail. They had suspicions that the enemy might use the addresses for propaganda purposes.

Another move was planned. It was to be a six-hour journey. We planned to shove off at noon. Spent the remainder of the morning packing things up. Light snow again, flurries, not enough to stall our efforts.

We made the move south, about 60 miles on a twisting, muddy road. The journey would have been only 12 miles had the road been straight. We went down to Suwon, then over north of Wonju where we were told to hold until further notice, until Division Artillery called. We waited again for orders, slept when we could, wondered what was next. We knew there would be a big push soon. We prepared ourselves mentally for the move.

One could almost sense the nervousness in the air, the caustic anticipation that always surrounded a waiting army. My letters home were generally upbeat. If there was any bad news about us, I wanted them to get it from the papers, not from me. I continued to be as positive about my role as possible, assuring them that I was safe and sound, far enough in back of the front to be protected.

Moved again at 12:30 the next day. We were on the road until

16:30. Found ourselves in the middle of a wet rice paddy somewhere near Wonju in the 1st Cavalry sector. Heard they would move to the East the following day, as would the 24th Division. They were narrowing the sectors and the 3rd Division and we were filling the gap. As it stood, from the West Coast, we had the ROK, the Turks, British, U.S. 3rd, U.S. 25th, 1st Cavalry, U.S. 24th and the U.S. 2nd Division. I had no idea what was on the East Coast. All we did was wait around and sweat it out until all the moving was over, when we would stabilize and have a line we could depend on.

The 1st Cavalry and the 25th Division (Lightning Division) were side by side when the Chinese entered the war. I was told, when the charge came, the Chinese split the U.S. Army in half. All units on the Western front retreated down the Red Dog Highway toward Kaesong and Seoul. The 1st Calvary infantry apparently retreated without letting the 8th FA know of the action. They were on the left flank of the 8th Army. It was called "bugging out" in Army slang. Some said the black stripe on the 1st Cavalry patch represented the split lines when they pulled back against the onslaught. At least that's what the 8th FA believed.

We had one crew sleeping in CP. No real shifts. Men were awakened whenever they were needed.

No mail. Being on the move really fouled things up. Every time they moved the APO it took a few days to get things back to normal. They did a good job despite the setbacks. Every morning the agent left with outgoing mail, picked up whatever mail he could at the APO and then returned to battalion headquarters, where they broke down the mail. That was usually where the foul-up occurred. They had no real facility in which to sort the mail. They kept it in the battalion mail jeep. The boxes were few; they were sorted first. Then the letters. It was remarkable how well the mail came through. It had top priority, next to chow.

February 16: We moved on line again in support of the 27th Infantry, into a village named So Sangnon Ni, about five miles west of Wonju.

I received a letter from Roy who lived in Black Duck, Minnesota. He was in the 25th Recon Company. He went through training with me at Fort Lewis. He told me two of his pals were missing and presumed to be dead after the retreat through Seoul, one we called Satch, Eugene, from Missouri and another named Wesley from Rochester, Minnesota. It brought to mind how lucky I was to be in my outfit, doing a job that kept me out of danger for the most part.

My clumsiness was the brunt of many jokes ever since the night I tripped over the tongue of a trailer being pulled by a ¾-ton truck. The fact that I had night blindness, the inability to adjust quickly from a lighted condition to a darkened condition, didn't convince any of my buddies that it was an accident. Even Bob Schranck, who knew about my problem, couldn't abstain from poking fun at me.

The problem was highlighted one night when I was coming off duty. Our sleeping room was in one of the local houses and the night was exceptionally dark, cloudy, no moon. Now the Koreans all have a "honeybucket" buried to the left or right side of their front door. The "honeybucket" was their crude way of collecting and storing human waste until it could be spread in the rice fields as fertilizer. Returning to the house that evening, I did not see the buried bucket. I stepped right into the middle of it with one leg, right up to my crotch. My scream brought the boys running. I never heard so much laughter.

They didn't let me back in the house until I had stripped off my pants and washed myself off. Even then the smell lingered. I put on some clean clothes, crawled into the sack, and suffered the indignity of a bad accident. The next morning I burned the fouled clothes.

It was standard operating procedure for us to have a firing plan ready that included a great many rounds to fire on target, to soften it up prior to a scheduled advance. That was the case when the 27th jumped off on the 17th of February. We fired about 1,000 rounds prior to 9:00 when they started to go forward. The FOs that were with them screamed back coordinates so fast that we could hardly keep up with them. The weather was bad on the front. We pounded, pounded, pounded them relentlessly for most of the day, firing 3,500 rounds in all. It was a tough, tough fight, as good as could be expected with all the Chinese facing them. Toward the end of the day they reported a tremendous number of enemy dead with little loss to themselves. We were pleased that we had done our job well, that we had saved American lives. Sometimes, even in the middle of a war, there were things to be thankful for.

The weather turned bad again. Snow and hard winds. Sharp cold.

We had our big tent up. Our FDC was in a Korean house, one of the warmest rooms in a long time. We learned that our new FDC truck would be along soon, smaller and compact, with everything we needed to operate smoothly. It would also end the practice of making the FDC the officers' dayroom. It was not uncommon to have six officers and three men in FDC, when all we should have had were five enlisted men and one officer. The heat and light just drew those officers in like flies to a picnic.

Had a stroke of luck. One of the boys in the survey section noticed a pair of boots in the ditch when he was on guard. They were a size 13M, with rubber bottom and leather tops, complete with a felt insole, great for warmth. He remembered that I had a big hole in mine so he brought them over. They fit. I then had an extra pair. With the new boots, and four pair of socks, I was all fixed to keep my feet warm.

I reached for a whole stack of letters from home on the same day we received our new 6 × 6 FDC truck. When it came we transferred all our equipment into the new traveling house so we would be ready to work when we moved to our next position. The new truck replaced the one we had to load and unload every time we moved. It had a big HCO table across one end, with drawers under the table and radios on the wall within easy reach. The right side wall had the plotting board and situation map. A small stove was located just inside the door on the left. Telephones were wired to a common connection point outside the truck for easy connection by the wire crews. The working space was small, but by having two shifts, it cut out excess people. Above all, it couldn't be the officers' dayroom any more. It was for work and nothing else.

The new truck proved to be a godsend when we moved twice in two days. The first move was short because of the bad roads. Snow again. Temperatures about 15 degrees. Cold as a well-digger's ass, so they say. Spent the night outdoors in my sleeping bag, snuggled inside. Was barely able to keep warm. Getting up and getting dressed were the worst parts. I missed the Korean shacks.

Moved again into a dry riverbed. We were able to put up the big squad tent and a stove for heat, a generator for lights. The truck was easy. All we had to do was wait for the wire crew to hook us up and we were in business, first with the radio connections, then with the rest. I learned that we were on the Kyongan-chi-On riverbed, about six miles from where it joined the Han. They told us we would move again for the third day in a row, closer to the Han where we would set up in buildings. Not too soon for any of us. By that time we looked like we belonged to the "House of David." Unlike the officer facilities, we had to wait for the right setup in order to get hot water and find a place out of the cold to wash and shave. Dogfaces didn't get any of the perks. We had to wait until conditions were right.

After the move we were situated in what used to be a school, now nothing more than a bombed-out shell. The officers picked out the good houses and we got the rest. The school must have been nice at one time. They had a large schoolyard, big classrooms with windows, blackboards, and all the necessary study facilities. It appeared as though the students worked on very low seats, behind tables such as I remember from the first grade. Everything was wrecked. Most of the facility was damaged beyond use. I figured when they eventually opened it again the entire thing would have to be replaced. Such a sorry sight. It made me wonder about the very concept of war. Certainly there must be a better way to resolve differences rather than through death and destruction. How beautiful my memories were then, as I stared through the vacant burned-out rooms, the idyllic street on which I lived, my own school, clean and colorful, the laughter, the freshness of our seasons, the freedom we shared. All in all, I guess it was the freedom for which we fought, our right to enjoy the fine things, freedom from want and fear, our precious way of life.

Fired three rounds on an old concentration. The rounds were right on target. A new fellow with us didn't raise a finger to help with the mission. He just looked at us, expected us to do the work. He was a staff sergeant. We had no time for him. Frenchy and I got the rounds off by ourselves even though it took a while longer. The Major was sleeping in the truck, but he woke up fast when the guns sounded. He asked what we were doing. We told him we were answer-

FDC TRUCK. Richard Holmsten (left), horizontal control operator [HCO] and later chief of section, and Sefton Stallard, vertical control operator [VCO], standing in front of the new truck with an enclosed housing on top of the steel truck body. This shelter contained the required chart table, the radio and telephone stations, lights and ventilation fan so that when we moved into position our fire direction center was ready to operate either by radio first and then telephone to the forward observers and other firing batteries of our battalion. This shelter made it possible for us to be ready to assist the infantry quickly. Before this truck was constructed it was necessary first to locate the fire direction center and then arrange for lights and security for the members of the center.

ing an urgent call from the Forward Observer. He nodded. More than ever, I had a soft spot in my heart for the FOs.

That night I had to log in a report from the Rangers. They had tried to cross our sector of the Han but didn't make it. No casualties reported on my watch. But I imagined there would be some when my relief took over. As for the Rangers, they were the best of the best, always putting their lives on the line for an objective. Gutsy guys—bravery runs in their blood.

It rained as we prepared to cross the Han. It started in the morning and kept up all day. Heavy rain. Steady. Drops the size of quarters. The temperature was up to about 40 degrees. The snow all but disappeared under the constant downpour. Mud would be our next obstacle. The roads would be grease, axle-hugging gumbo that would surely slow us down. We were living in front of the gun batteries. That resulted in noise and concussion, as all the rounds were going directly overhead on a low trajectory. Even so, we rarely detected the smell of gunpowder in the air.

The 27th Infantry went off line and we went on direct support for the Turks again. They are good at what they do, so we didn't worry much about the Chinese getting the best of them. The constant firing was beginning to wear on us. Racket all the time. Little opportunity for a good sleep. We had one battery on each side of us and one behind firing directly overhead. We were sleeping in what was left of a tin building. It was like sleeping inside a drum.

The Han River continued to hold us back. By January 22, all the infantry units were shifting personnel. Fresh men were coming in. The buildup was starting. We all knew an offensive would begin soon.

Fired 20 different missions of time on target. TOT really made an impression on us. The sheer power of all that destruction landing on one spot at the same time, without warning, had to be the most demoralizing thing the enemy faced. How lucky we were to be delivering that rain of death, rather than receiving it.

Had a lull in the firing. Got all packed up, then were told to hold everything. We didn't fire a single round for an entire day. Our boys were coming down off the hills. They said we cleaned off our side of the river.

I enjoyed a full night's sleep, then moved again the following day. The roads were terrible. The winter weather really took its toll on the road surfaces. They were pocked with chuckholes, potholes, shellholes, mud, rocks, everything that shouldn't have been there. The Red Dog Highway was a step above other roads, but even that was hard going. Moving forward was a slow and cautious effort. The rain didn't help. We had to wait for the engineers to drain off a spot so we could move forward.

Mail was still fouled up. APO was having as much difficulty getting organized as were the other units. I was eager to get mail. I was waiting for my OCS application. When the mail finally did come I read and re-read my letters. Just as I finished, we received nine harassing missions from Division and had to get the data down to the three batteries quickly. The missions, on enemy concentrations, were crucial. We put down fire on the points all night at the rate of about three rounds per battalion per hour, 18 rounds per hour from our outfit alone. The Division staggered the timing of the rounds through most of the night. The tension diminished toward dawn. The remaining firing then was not done in panic.

Just as the sun was coming up, Schranck came bouncing past me in a ¾-ton truck and asked if I was dirty enough for a shower. He said he was going to the shower unit, over by the Turks. It didn't take any persuasion to get my attention. I hopped into the truck and we started off overland. We picked up three more guys on the way. When we told them where we were going, we didn't get a single negative reply. After taking the shower, I slipped into some clean clothes and stood in for an inspection. Felt like a new man. Wonderful things, soap and water.

Went into the hills with our rifles for a bit of target practice. Worked up an appetite. When we returned we found that "A" rations were available. Excellent food. Time off for sleep and relaxation, a break from the steady firing that often lasted 20 hours a day.

The respite didn't last long. Moved again. Set up a new base point. Fired continuously with 12 batteries, defensive fire at points where a counter-charge could occur. A testy time. Defensive fire was used to beat back enemy attacks and to make sure we had a way out if their push was successful.

Stallard received his OCS papers in the mail. Mine didn't come. We both talked to the major. He said we might have a chance if everything went well, if we got past the Army red tape. The personnel sergeant, on the other hand, said our chances were very poor. His opposition was expected. He was intent on looking at his man count. He wasn't about to let the core of the FDC leave unless replacements arrived first. He would only be willing to get us commissions if we were willing to go "on the hill" with the infantry FOs. When it came down to getting a battlefield commission, I would have had to extend my duty in Korea 90 days past the scheduled rotation date and agree to be an FO. When put to me in that manner, I suddenly became uninterested.

Mail came again. Mail sure quiets the waters. Letters and pictures to warm the soul.

I got involved in a poker game, lost some money. I had no business in the game, but I stayed for a couple of hours. Beyond that, too much money was involved. The change of activity did prove one thing, however. I didn't belong in that group of men.

Payday followed my losses. I decided not to draw any money out, but to let it build up until I had enough to send home. No need for money on the front lines. Too many fast fingers. Few were trustworthy.

The Rangers were out again on a kill or be killed mission across the Han. They picked a black night for the mission. It was as dark as the inside of a coalmine. Good for their type of work.

The offensive was near. We could all feel it, like electricity in the air.

11

THE HAN OFFENSIVE

Operation RIPPER began on March 7 with one of the most concentrated artillery barrages of the Korean War, preparing for the crossing of the Han by the 25th Division. Their purpose? To establish a bridgehead on the north bank. The assault was launched at dawn. Chinese defenders north of the Han fled under a rain of 50,000 shells and heavy air support. It was a turning point in the war. A battalion of the famous 27th Wolfhound Regiment paced the attack at two points east of Seoul, hitting the Red side in three waves as other American elements surged across to their left and right.

We were part of the concentrated effort, a total of 148 artillery pieces, 100 tanks, hundreds of mortars and machine guns that turned loose on the Chinese that fateful day. At the time we were in direct support of the 27th Infantry, which was part of the 25th Division. The 8th FA had three firing batteries of six howitzers (Abel, Baker, and Charlie batteries).

The day began with a normal communication from the forward observer. Our call sign, Fandango-3, this is Wolf-eye Abel, was assigned to FO by the infantry and given to us from regimental. We changed our call signs frequently but always ended up with 3, as it was our designated FDC number. Once wire was laid, each FO had a telephone line connected to the infantry switchboard and from there to us.

When a FO opened a line between himself and us, it was a dedicated line, not to be cut off. The infantry switchboard became a major connection point because it was connected to each FO and also to each company commander. The switchboards operated between themselves. When we wanted to talk to Division we went through the 8th FA Battalion switchboard.

"Fandango-3. This is Wolf-eye. Do you read me?"

"Fandango-3 to Wolf-eye, here. Go ahead."

"Fire mission. We have activity near the intersection of the work roads marked Main and Extra. Requesting fire to pin them down."

"Roger. Stand by. We'll have rounds on the way shortly."

The FO replied. "Wake the boys up. This looks like a busy day for the infantry."

"Roger."

As HCO operator it was my job to first locate the requested target and set up the basic information as to distance and direction. The charges set were HE, high explosive.

The VCO operator in contact with the battery announced the charge, the deflection change from the base point as announced by the HCO and the elevation based on yardage. The VCO then announced the number of rounds. He would then announce, "Fire!"

The gun batteries applied this data after ramming the two-part round home into the howitzer charged with five powder bags. The breech plate was then slammed shut, and the gunner would fire.

"On the way!" The intensive barrage had begun.

We fired, fired, fired, on that bright sunny morning as the 25th moved out across the Han in a line of green assault boats, each carrying ten men and two engineers who brought the boats back for more men. They paddled with long, wooden oars, as fast as they could, across the murky water. Their objective was to secure a beachhead, behind the steady roar of explosives ripping the ground ahead of them, our rounds softening up the enemy. It was a time of great concern. Many lives were on the line. We worked hard, fast, accurately, to provide them with the best cover they could get. We cheered when we heard that it was quiet on the opposite shore, surprisingly quiet. Had we successfully subdued the enemy? It appeared we had. Our men had gained ground. They had taken the first objective. We were washed with success, there in FDC, for we had done our part and had done it well. We had saved lives, and had given the enemy reason to worry.

It had been our task to provide a softening fire of the area that was defended by the Chinese and North Korean armies. The FOs had reported that protective cover had been constructed on the north shore. It had been our mission to destroy that cover before the crossing started. Our men would be open targets on the water, very exposed, without cover. It was our job to eliminate that threat. It was a tense time for us in the 8th because we knew that the 27th depended on our accuracy. I wouldn't say we were frantic but we were concerned, knowing that our accuracy had to be perfect. If it wasn't and if the bridgehead failed to materialize, we would be right in the lap of the Chinese and North Koreans, not a very comfortable position. This was the big push. Everyone knew it. The engineers' construction equipment was parked all around the area and along every road. Jeeps with flags showing the rank of the officers were running everywhere. Everyone was wondering when the offensive would start.

Our position that day was in front of the firing batteries but behind the infantry headquarters and infantry companies. They were spread out across the terrain at every useable spot, living in small tents and small assembly areas. We actually didn't come in close contact with the infantry but were aware of the mass and the activity. There didn't seem to be any attempt to be secret about what was coming. The only question was, when?

Twenty-four hours before the jump-off hour the noise started. We were all in our position and ready. We could hear the 155 Long Toms boom close behind us. The shells went directly overhead, whoosh, whoosh, whoosh, like the cars of a fast moving train. The power was immense.

The tension mounted as we got close to the jump-off time. It was then we had to lift our fire and move it farther inland, off the beach. We had to be correct or we would drop our rounds on the infantry. The FOs kept us appraised at all times of our fire pattern. They could not control the big guns except to holler, to raise the fire if our boys were moving in under it. We cheered when the first messages came back. "We've reached the beach. They have bugged out." It meant that the Chinese had offered very little resistance. Our vicious softening fire had turned them back and saved the infantry from counting up their wounded and KIAs. Smiles all around.

We crossed the Han one day behind the infantry, at 13:00 hours, and set up right on the beach. The entire area was strewn with junk, shell holes, dead bodies left behind by the retreating Chinese. The buildings were shambles, no standing structures of any kind. Aid stations had been moved in well before we arrived. Wounded were arriving in ambulances. The Chinese were being buried by the hundreds. We had taken numerous prisoners. The activity on the beachhead was amazing—trucks, tanks, boats, tents—as if the entire American army had been spilled on one spot.

Within hours after the crossing, the engineers had put up a fine pontoon bridge and a walking bridge. The bridge was comprised of large, inflated black pontoons. The top of each pontoon was about two to three feet above the water level. The length was long enough so when placed at right angle to a vehicle there was room for two tracks, which the trucks followed as a roadway. The narrow walking bridge was for single file passage only and was set up alongside the main bridge. The pontoons were floated into place and lashed together side by side, forming a path of heavy, strong roadway supports from shore to shore for the trucks to drive on.

The beachhead was all sand, about two football fields in length. From that point on the land rose up in a gradual green landmass: no large hills, cliffs or any predominant landmarks. We went across as part of headquarters battery, behind the infantry. The battery commanders were directed to spread left and right from the discharge point on the sand and direct the howitzers to set up on the riverbank pointing north, spreading their tow bars and digging in for firing. It involved spacing our 18 howitzers along the beach in three groups of six, to form a battery. Our location was beyond the beach on firm ground, in front of the guns and out of the way. We were not in a protected area but reports indicated no enemy forces nearby. The howitzers came quickly after the headquarters' group and the battery locations were assigned.

We did a lot of firing from the riverbank while waiting for the other two regiments to get up on line so we were not vulnerable to encirclement. When we got the truck set up above the beach, we worked with a new set of regulations. For safety and security purposes, a sentry was stationed right outside the truck door. In order to get in, the sentry would pound on the door to alert us. It was then the choice of those inside to either shut off the lights and open the door, tell the sentry to hold until they completed their tasks, or take a chance with a quick in-out opening and closing. The main concern at the time of the crossing was whether the intelligence reports of enemy strength were accurate. Did they have large numbers of troops hidden that could compromise our position? Had the UN troops provided adequate protection? Could the Chinese have made plans for an ambush? Fortunately, the crossing barrage had done the job. The Chinese were never there in numbers. They had pulled back in the face of the concentrated fire.

Prior to the big push we had been on an ammunition ration. Once the barrage started and the cover fire was in place, the talk of ammo ration was never discussed. We fired all we had and got more as needed. The supply of ammo was nonstop once the push had started. When the crossing was completed, the rear guard supply got into the act and shut down our nonregulation firing. From that point on it was a wait and see proposition.

Actually we ran out of targets. Once we got set up across the Han we were in a holding position, waiting for the infantry to stabilize the lines. The one thing we did not want was the Chinese to break through a bulge and get us into an entrapment situation. We had no targets for a few days.

During that time my aggressive toothache, which I had been suppressing for days with aspirin, began to act up big time. During the barrage and the crossing, the dentist was nowhere to be found. Only after we set up and were in a holding position did I receive permission from the captain to look up the dentist. I was taken across the pontoon by jeep. MPs were everywhere, controlling the passage of vehicles. The experience of leaving my unit and finding a dentist in the middle of a field, with a chair and a treadle arrangement for a drill, was something that is still hard to believe. The medical corps had many different services to help the GIs in addition to bandaging wounds. When it came to assisting the troops on the ground, the U.S. Army was truly amazing.

When I walked in, I was surprised to find that the dental assistant was David, a fellow I got to know aboard the ship. He was one of the fellow KPs who was studying to be a chiropractor in Indiana. He recognized me as soon as I walked into the tent. He told me he had volunteered to be a dental assistant. I told him I was in the 8th Artillery, across the river.

He snapped a towel around my neck, laid me back on the headrest, told me to open up. I spread my mouth. He peered in while stating his opinion of the war. We talked about ten minutes before the dentist came in, hustling David aside.

I spent an entire day at the dental tent, about one hour in the chair. They found an infected wisdom tooth, a lower one, way in back, covered by gum and bone. He worked hard on it, removed it in one piece. While he worked on me, he removed teeth from three other men. Assembly-line dentistry.

I sat in a three-legged chair with a back and a headrest. David ran the drill, like a sewing machine. It was crude, but did the job. I was lucky to have a dentist so close.

After having my teeth fixed, I was lucky enough to eat lunch at Division Artillery. The food was excellent. They even had mustard and ketchup, jam for their bread. I used David's mess kit, had all the food I could carry. He told me they had two generals to feed, which was the reason they got the best of incoming rations. They also didn't move very often.

I hitched a ride back in an infantry jeep. The driver was a young kid, not more than 18. He drove like a madman. He had a different outlook on the war. He said he was lucky that some of his buddies got hit. It gave him a chance to drive in recon. Now he didn't have to walk. He had wheels. His job was to drive fast, to find the enemy and report their positions. He considered himself a spy for the infantry.

When I mentioned that his job sounded dangerous, he shrugged, kept his eyes on the road, said he nearly got hit three times. He wasn't concerned about going home in a body bag. He just wanted to get hit in the leg or the arm, just enough to get a ticket home. His constant talk convinced me that even a sane man can get goofy after a while, given the noise and horror of war.

He dropped me at the pontoon bridge, wheeled the jeep around and skidded back down the road, his engine roaring. I just shook my head and started walking.

I had taken only a few steps on the bridge with a few other

soldiers when the MPs came dashing toward me, yelling for us to get off the bridge. When we asked what was wrong, he said some dummy started a fire.

Sure enough. Near the center of the bridge, a pontoon was ablaze. The MPs forced us back to shore. We stood and watched as others rushed to extinguish it.

We learned later that one of the men got cold and filled an empty Number-10 food container with gasoline then lighted it. When he attempted to move it he grabbed the top rim, burned his fingers and threw it in the river upstream. It floated downstream, got caught up under the pontoon where it exploded. Before the fire was out it had ruptured three of the pontoons. All travel stopped. The brass were unhappy. The MP at fault was chewed out. We sat on the bank and waited, watched the show.

They cut the burning pontoons loose, allowed them to float away with the current, into deeper water, where they sank. Spare pontoons were brought up, floated beneath the ramp, fixed into position. The whole thing took about two hours.

Shortly after midnight on the 10th of March, while we were still set up on the riverbed doing a firing mission, a reporter from the Edward R. Murrow show (NBC) walked into our truck and identified himself. He had a PRESS badge pinned to his chest. He carried a recorder. He asked permission to have it on while we worked. The officer in charge nodded his approval and we went about our business as if he wasn't there.

His first questions were directed at the officers. They gave him the usual canned reply, threw in a lot of military jargon that normal civilians wouldn't understand. Frenchy and I sat back and listened, didn't think he'd ask us anything.

To my surprise, when he finished with the officers, he leaned over my plotting board and asked if I would answer a few questions. With thoughts of the woman reporter still in my head, I had an inclination to be uncooperative. But the officers were there, so I told him what he wanted to know, my name, where I was from, a brief background on how I came to Korea, some information about our unit, nothing he couldn't use on the air. It seemed trite to me. Who would ever understand what I said? Who would care? My words would be narrowed down to just a few, to add "reliability" to the piece, if they were used at all. Frenchy, our radio operator, added some comment. Nothing was said about our personal opinions of the war. Even if it had been, it would have been deleted. When he was finished I asked when the piece was going to be on the air.

His answer was direct. It would probably air either on March 16 or the 23rd. He said it would take some editing, piecing together, would probably end up to be about a 30-second clip. Murrow liked to keep things concise, but clear. It would probably broadcast about 20:00 our time. I told him we'd probably be firing. We usually were. The officers nodded. The reporter said he would make sure the listeners understood the key role our unit played in the Han offensive.

After the interview, the reporter drove away in his private jeep. I was sure he had deadlines to keep. We went back to work.

I wrote Florence and told her about the event. I never found out if Murrow did broadcast our interview. If he did, no one back home heard it.

Pulled out again. Moved up north of the river, on the Punkam, about three miles from the big loop. Things were quiet for two days. The infantry was on the move but very slow. They took objectives one at a time, cautiously. We laid down fire whenever they called. The sergeant was on the radio, Stallard on plot. We would get the infantry location and plot the "no fire line" from Division. The sergeant continued his verbal assault on us, his personal weapon. He made no secret that he disliked the Reserves and never let any of us forget it, despite our proficiency on the job. His big mouth was always open, never praising, always criticizing. Once again, the captain and the major had their hands full, keeping him in line. It led to some very unpleasant moments.

I was on duty for the last mission, when the front line was spread east and west about 3,000 yards north. On the plot board, we had north-south lines dividing the sectors, or sections, of infantry regiments or companies. The sector lines could also divide regiments or divisions, appropriate to their deployment. When we received coordinates on a mission from FO, the first thing I checked was the situation map to be sure it was in a sector within our assigned area. No mistakes. Everything had to be perfect. Our boys up front had little room for error. Sometimes I think the first sergeant was actually proud of our work, although he never admitted it. But we could see the hidden pride in his eyes whenever we received a pat on the back. His gritty, sewer mouth was used most often when the officers weren't present.

I returned to Division Artillery for another dental check. They found six more holes in my teeth, said I would be a regular customer as long as I was conveniently located. David cleaned my teeth. I felt much better when it was over. When I returned I got my share of the workload. Having been gone all day, they worked me from 19:00 hours right through midnight.

A quiet night. The infantry were beyond our range. They had moved farther than we could fire. We were sure to move again the following day, two miles west, twenty miles south, then up the other side of a small bald-topped mountain—a long trip for such a short distance. Thankfully the Koreans were busy repairing all the roads for troop movements. They worked by the thousands, carrying earth, sand, rocks, anything to fill shell holes, to smooth out ruts and to strengthen the road surfaces. But despite their work, the roads were still poor.

We moved as planned. The weather was warmer, the sun bright on some days. The snow was melting. Water drained down the ditches in small streams. Mud was everywhere, which made for hard travel. The Koreans couldn't do much with the mud. They kept throwing in rocks.

We were quiet for a couple of days. Walked around without our jackets. Spring in the air. The smell of damp earth reminded me of home, like Minnesota in thaw. Breezes still chilly with winter. The sun warm on my face.

On a fine spring afternoon, Frenchy, Stallard and I took off walking into the hills, far enough away to be out of earshot from the activity. We found a place on one of the south slopes amid some scrub brush and sat down, looked out over the terrain, saw nothing but hills sweeping off to the south, dull colored, broken, shattered trees, the remnants of war clearly visible. It was quiet. Stallard lit a cigarette. His smoke stalled momentarily before being lifted away by a light breeze. Frenchy sprawled full out on his back, his eyes to the sky. No one spoke for a time. We all had our inner thoughts. Mine were centered on home, on a day when Florence and I had sat atop Barn Bluff, above Red Wing, gazing out over the Mississippi River. I almost didn't hear Frenchy's voice. He asked me when the war would be over.

How was I to know. It was Stallard who answered. He thought it would be the next year, when we pushed them back over the 38th Parallel. We were getting stronger by the day. Soon we'd have them at a disadvantage. They would see the futility of it all. Stalemates, he said, didn't win wars.

I said I just wanted to get home. Everything would be greening soon. Baseball season was about to start. Frenchy scoffed, said I didn't have enough mud on my boots yet. Stallard brushed a fly from his face, said he could wait for rotation. Frenchy again, reminding us that rotation was just a nice way of saying that someone else would take our bullet.

Frenchy lit another cigarette. Stallard dozed almost to the point of snoring. Out and away I heard the drone of a plane, the sudden cough of an engine. When I closed my eyes it wasn't unlike that Sunday on Barn Bluff. Again, my memory took me back.

On the way back we stopped at one of the gun batteries, found Mr. Fixit by accident, talked to him for a while. Before my watch hit 15:00 we were back at our unit.

I took my clothes to an old Mama-san for washing. She told me I'd get them back the next day. Hopefully we wouldn't move before then. Wet or dry, we'd pull out. If they did come back wet, I'd stuff them in a waterproof bag until I could dry them. The dry clothes I could put in my bedroll.

I shaved and washed. Card games in the Medic tent. Radio on. Music once again. Schranck, Stallard, Little Joe, Frenchy, Art Schwerin and a guy named Don played canasta. Light rain on the canvas. Laughter and curses. Good losers and bad. Felt the need for home stronger than ever.

We moved again, west of the Punkam, into a low valley. Light fog in the early morning hour just before sunrise. Stallard and I had our own canvas shelter, quieter, away from the noise of the big tent.

AT EASE. The core group of this narrative was relaxing on a quiet day in reserve. *Left to right, back row:* Jimmy (Regular Army) from the wire and communication section; Richard Holmsten (Reserve) HCO (and Chief of Section); Joseph (Little Joe) Quartararo (Regular Army), radio and communications operator assigned to this FDC. *Middle row:* Sefton Stallard (Reserve) (VCO); Rod Scheffer (Reserve), radio operator assigned to the survey section. *Front:* Bob Schranck (Reserve) (VCO) and survey section. When there was time, this is the group that gathered for relaxation and conversation. When we were busy all of us rotated in all the FDC stations even though our assignment may have been in a specific section. The FDC required all of us to work together at one time or another as a functioning unit.

Our OCS papers arrived. Captain Matt called Stallard and me into his tent. He greeted us with a smile, put us at ease, proceeded to give us the news about our wild request for OCS. His smile turned to a smirk as he reminded us that nothing is stable. Things always change.

Stallard and I glanced at one another, both expecting the worst. He went on to say that this pipe dream of ours, to get out of the unit, would never happen, unless we had a magic way to rapidly educate and train replacements. That was it. Dead end. My shoulders sagged.

The captain continued, said we could expect to be held in the active army and the artillery. The Army wouldn't allow us to transfer from an important job in FDC just so we could go home. Even if we did get into OCS, it would be preceded by a stint of duty as a forward observer at the pleasure of the Army. Then it would be an additional two years of active service. He also thought it unlikely that they would discharge surplus officers like they did after World War II.

I nodded. Stallard did the same. He tried to convince us that it would be to our advantage to simply stay where we were until our length of service was up and not go looking for something that would only get us in deeper water.

Obviously, I had a disgruntled look on my face. He asked me if I understood. I said I did. He smiled again, that varnished mark of superiority. He concluded by saying that neither I or Stallard were Regular Army material. As he saw it, we were simply uniformed civilians.

That was the end of our OCS hopes. The Captain's explanation was clear enough. We'd have to wait it out.

Back on the night shift. Peace and quiet for a change. A chance to write letters, sleep until noon. Things were slow. We fired 25 rounds during the day at a range of 11,000 yards, or 6.25 miles. Although we didn't know what the target was, we worked in close contact with the FO. The Chinese had pulled back. We suspected a plane had spotted a target and had located it by coordinates and not by objective.

Cold and windy again. Tried to stay inside as much as possible. Caught up on my sleep. I neglected to shave because the stove was a long way from where Stallard and I were perched. We expected to move again to the main east-west road about 15 miles out of Seoul, behind a hill that would provide good protection. The new location would get us right in the middle of things again, unless the infantry continued to move north, pushing the enemy out of range. They were moving north at a steady pace. It was difficult keeping up with them.

A division artillery general came through and notified us that about 7,000 troops were on their way to Korea. That, we thought, could start rotation in a big way. Until then most of the replacements used in the Korean conflict were reservists, to fill the ranks of those injured or killed. Rotation was all about building points. Lucky for me, I was married. That counted for points. Being in an on-line outfit was another point-building factor. R&R to Japan was a negative, therefore I never bucked for R&R. Schranck had been in Japan, in both the hospital and for rest and relaxation. He had lost points. If rotation was going to kick in, it was another good reason not to push for OCS.

Stallard talked the medics out of a salamander heater. Warmth for our tent.

Chinese propaganda came to us via a male radio announcer we dubbed Peking Boy. He spoke English as fluently as any native American. He was the equivalent of Tokyo Rose who talked to our troops during the Second World War. His standard broadcasts inferred that we were all puppets for the politicians, that we should revolt against our officers and that we should all lay down our arms and refuse to fight the North Koreans who had a legitimate claim to the territory. I never thought his broadcasts would do anything other than make us laugh. But my opinion changed when one of our boys, a young guy named Jimmy, actually began believing the propaganda. He was a small, skinny kid with a pockmarked face who was afraid of his own shadow. The voice on the radio really bothered him. Being far from home, lonesome and as homesick as a lost cat, he was never far from a physical or mental breakdown. He was one of the boys who seldom received mail. It was always a pity to see the faces of those who never got mail, the forgotten ones. They were ripe for the propaganda and whenever it came, it took a toll on their morale. Self-inflicted wounds were not uncommon.

It was Schranck's idea to make Welsh rabbit. He knew I had a half loaf of my mother's rye bread. He had some cheese. After a short trip to the mess, he returned with five pounds of oleo and a can of mixed salt and pepper. He also knew I had a can of beer in my bag and had no particular use for it. He said they were the perfect ingredients for Welsh rabbit. On his section's cooking stove, he melted the oleo and the cheese and added a small amount of beer and seasoning. When that was melted together, forming a thick paste, he poured it over the toasted rye bread. It was a new way to have toasted cheese sandwiches, which was my definition of the concoction. I also had a can of British sweets that contained five bars of bittersweet chocolate. We chopped that up and added cocoa powder and sugar, made fudge for desert. Even though it didn't harden too well, it was sugary and delicious. Besides having good fun, we also had good chow. The only casualties were Bob's mess kit and my canteen cup, which served as our pans.

We hustled to move again. The Intelligence boys expected our sector to be hit because of a troop shift. We had another division on line with us and our hopes were that they'd stall out at the 38th parallel rather than try to wipe out the entire Chinese army. It seemed ludicrous to think that we'd end Communism by this "police action." Stop their incursion, yes. But irradicating their form of government, no. Fight. Kill. Maim. It seemed to be the only way to solve differences, and the situation caused more blood to flow every day. God knows how many we killed with our barrages: hundreds, perhaps thousands. No way of knowing.

We fired until 21:00.

When I returned to the tent, I found that Schranck had received a can of unpopped corn. No reason to go to bed. We stayed up, popped the corn, devoured it all, went to work again at midnight.

The Chinese hit our lines at 05:00, with bugles blowing. We fired a frantic 800 rounds and put down the attack. About a half hour later they hit us again. There were some anxious moments until we put about 30 rounds right in the middle of a group of 200. They regrouped and tried again.

Our FO had a hair-raising few hours until he finally radioed, "Bingo! You did it that time. Great shooting. Pass the word on to the gun crews. Thanks for being with us."

Then everything settled down. I got a few hours' sleep. Being overrun was always a fear, especially when we were not supporting the 27th, who had a good record of protecting their artillery.

March 24 brought another lull in the fighting. Some of our guys returned from R&R. It appeared as though they had bought out the entire whiskey supply in Japan. Most were hung over. A few were still drunk. Two of them were supposed to pull a shift with me but they were out of order. I worked until 21:00 and was back again at midnight for another two and a half hours. We fired about 1,300 rounds in that short period of time in support of the infantry who had moved into "no-man's" land.

I had to straighten out the records because two of the men were sick. So were the officers. One had passed out, had to be carried to his quarters. Another was carried to his tent against his will. Still another drank.

One sergeant from the radio section and another code man got so drunk they decided to shoot up the place. With their pistols blazing, they shot ten new holes in the squad tent. It was one of the reasons Stallard and I chose to sleep in a pup tent. You could never count on a good night's sleep with any of those boozeheads. A can of beer usually lasted me about two weeks. I preferred soda pop.

The next morning the battery commander lined us all up against the truck. He was fuming mad, his face as red as a billiard ball. He shouted right in the faces of those who had created the furor the night before, said they had made fools of themselves and a fool of him. Someone could have been killed. Our men are important, he emphasized. We don't need them in the hospital because you dunderheads can't hold your liquor. He paced back and forth, chewing his words like the stub of a cigar, told them flat out that he was taking their stripes. He glared at the two men with a sneer that could frighten a mountain lion, said they were gun happy dummies that were going to pull extra duty until the day he returned. He added that this was to be a lesson for all of us. The next time anyone got sopped up on liquor and thought he was a one-man war, he'd end up in a stockade.

Easter Sunday. Quiet. The 27th was being returned to a rest area. They deserved it. We stayed on line to reinforce the fires of the

64th FA. There was no church service in our area. The chaplain came around at intervals, but not on Easter.

In an effort to break the work pattern and make Easter a special day, Division came by with a volleyball set. We cleared space for a court, chose teams. It was a good diversion. The fun and exercise were great even though we were a motley group, in combat boots, our carbines stacked alongside the makeshift court. We never ventured far away from our carbines. As the game picked up, our top shirts came off. We tried playing as well as we could. Rusty players on rough ground. Lots of tripping and falling. More shots were missed than were made. But we had a cheering section. It made us forget the war, if only for a little while.

The snow was disappearing fast. The once frozen ground had turned to mud. Weather reports indicated that we could expect rain. That meant real mud, hard travel, bogging down. It was amazing how fast the pile jackets and caps came off. I stuffed mine into my travel bag, changed from shoepack to combat boots as soon as the temperature climbed. It was not a smart move. As soon as the rain came, the mud increased. Then it was back to the waterproof snow packs because they offered the protection of rubber bottoms.

On the 25th they decided we should move again. We got the word at 14:00 just as rain came sloughing over the hills. We pulled into position in the middle of a downpour and by the time 17:00 rolled around it was a monsoon. It poured until 19:00 that night. When I finally came off duty it had stopped raining. I hit the sack and slept soundly until morning.

At 14:00 the next day we moved again, this time to a mountain pass. Hills on both sides squeezed our deployment. There was barely enough room to hold our FDC and gun sections. Rain came again, steady and unrelenting. Everything wet. It always rained for about 12 hours at a time, then turned to drizzle. The runoff created lakes in the rice paddies.

Living outside in tents or shelters by the guns was a matter of survival and the creative ability of the troops. I was amazed at how well the GIs protected themselves. Shelter halves were clipped together to form a roof. Big canvas covers were hard to find, but they showed up somehow. With the help of poles, they made good tent covers. When we were on the move, we seldom put up the squad tent because of the time and space required.

Rain, dreary rain. The ground a quagmire. The skies leaden. The morale, hopelessly dismal.

We moved again on the 26th and ended up in a fairly wooded area next to the 25th Recon platoon. Who was there but Roy, from Blackduck, Minnesota. When I saw him I threw my arms around his shoulder. I told him we thought he was killed in action when we retreated through Seoul in the middle of the night.

It was obvious Roy was glad to see me. He had been part of a group that took a wrong turn into a dead end street. They had been ambushed. When the firing started, he ran like hell, made it out okay. Some didn't. He got nicked. Lucky, he said. Wasn't until later that he got tangled up with a land mine that took down seven of them. Three went back to the States. He had spent a few weeks in the hospital with a mild concussion, not bad enough to send him home. As luck would have it, they threw him back on line. He was now taking care of a personnel carrier as a mechanic, part of Recon.

Recon traveled fast, in small groups, to find the enemy and report their positions to the infantry, told the FO where to expect resistance. He was glad to be out of the unit with a wrench in his hand. As a farm boy, he could fix anything. Mechanic was a good position for him.

We ate chow with his outfit, cooked food, steak, mashed spuds, peas, fruit, cookies and coffee. They ate well. I hoped we'd stay close so I could take advantage of their hospitality.

Went back to my outfit only to find meatballs and dehydrated potatoes. Learned that we'd move again the next day. So much for the good food.

More news about my OCS request. It seemed as though my records were fouled up and that my test grades were missing. So much for Army efficiency. I wrote it off as a lost cause, content to be what I was and where I was, hoping for early rotation.

As it was, memories of St. Paul thrived. There were frequent times when I was lost in melancholy. Mail came that had been written on Palm Sunday—another reason to think of home, the beauty of our land, the touch of my bride's hand, the melody of her voice, intensified by the distance. I felt alive and yearning in those moments of memory.

By the end of the month we were once again in support of the 27th Infantry. The war had suddenly pepped up. Our unit was on constant alert, as was the frontline. The colored boys in the 24th had taken 1,000 yards in three days. The 27th took their objective in 38 minutes and quickly got beyond our firing range. Two of the three gun batteries moved, leaving us to catch up. Things were much better with the 27th up front. The FOs knew exactly what was going on and when to call in fire.

The 24th Infantry Regiment was the unit that received all the publicity as being the first all-black unit, until they were split up by Harry S Truman. Desegregation was the best thing that ever happened to the Army. Prior to that, the 24th were victims of poor leadership. If an officer got involved in making poor command decisions, his punishment was to be transferred to the 24th. This could either be an infantry or an artillery outfit. We had an all-black artillery battalion in the 25th that supported the 24th just like we supported the 27th. Any infantry unit was no better than its leadership. The 24th had a reputation for questionable leadership. We never relaxed when we were in support of the 24th.

Our movie in the squad tent that afternoon was *Hit Parade of '51*. It wasn't the best film, but it gave us a look at the ladies. The newly acquired projector was a big improvement over the old wreck.

Quite often between 20:00 hours and 22:00 hours, we had a visit from "Bedcheck Charlie." He was the guy who flew a small airplane over our position at a low altitude and threw out hand grenades or small bombs to harass our sleep. His forays were seldom successful but he always gave us concern in case we were in the wrong place at the wrong time. He would generally make several passes on us, would collect ground fire from some of the perimeter guards and would then disappear north. I never heard if we ever shot "Charlie" down, or that he ever hit any troops. It just disturbed our night's sleep. In short, he was a pain in the ass.

I tried at times to put things into perspective, to find rational thoughts that would explain where I was and why I was there. It was never easy. Quite often I found myself reliving the journey and the stress and the fear, to reach no conclusion at all except to verify my existence as a soldier. Usually I remembered the landing ship, following the soldiers inland toward the assembly area, seeing my first visions of war, the shot-up railroad cars, the blank faces, the questioning stares. It was fear of the unknown that kept my nerves on edge, although being part of a group was always a steadying factor. I would always remember retreating across the Han in the darkness, with the mortars falling on both sides of the bridge, of Seoul in flames, its glow blazing like a hellfire across the sky. Being dressed in the same clothes for weeks. Driving in the dark toward some unknown destination. Rolling out my sack on the cold winter ground. Crawling into it, as if it were a safe haven, to protect me from all harm. Waking up with frost on the bag, teeth chattering, shoulders numb. The Chinese always seemed to know where we were. I thought at times they had eyes in the hills, ears in the night. Their presence was everywhere. Stallard was the one that kept me level. Relax, he'd always say. Let the brass worry. Schranck could sleep through anything. I would sometimes lay awake and wonder how the hell I was ever going to get home. Fortunately, loneliness was always diminished by letters, those marvelous messages that inevitably raised my morale.

The captain was always telling us stories about World War II. He was in the artillery where the battlefronts were much smaller than in Korea. He often said that many of the infantry fronts in Korea were comparable to division fronts in Europe. We were fortunate, he said. In Europe there was always incoming German artillery to match whatever our army threw at them. Round for round. The Germans, he said, were a rugged bunch. They knew how to fight a war.

Sometimes at night I would be jolted awake by the quad fifties cutting loose, .50 caliber machine guns mounted on half-tracks, for aircraft defense. If fired along the ground, they could cut down trees. The noise was deafening. They occasionally shot infiltrators. Despite their noise, we were always glad they were out there.

It was not unusual for me or any soldier to think about getting hit or killed. Death was constant. We dished it out, received it occasionally, even though we were a good distance behind the lines. There was always fear, like a lurking Jack-the-Ripper sneaking up behind you. Sleep was important, sack time being rare on occasions, between the firing, the moving, the working, the eating, the dogged routine, the bitching. Sleep came during the times between and it was seldom serene.

12

THE TIDE
TURNS AGAIN

April 1951: We were now 30 days past the crossing of the Han. History will confirm that after the crossing, the 8th FA advanced in a series of moves east and north in direct support of the infantry. This was clearly a time when the UN forces were trying to establish a fireline from east to west that could be moved north in a slow but steady manner. My role settled down to a routine diet of fire direction control and taking on the responsibility of chief of section in the FDC. The firefights that we had were to protect ourselves and the infantry from experiencing a breakthrough in the front that could put our battalion in the direct path of any advances by the Chinese or North Koreans.

It was also the time of year for weather changes from winter to spring, the rainy season, the eruption of the hot, stinky Korean summer. As the temperatures rose, the rice patties took on a smell that reeked with the foul stench of human waste. Honeybuckets that had been saved all winter were spread in the fields as a means of disposal and to fertilize the rice crop. In the winter it was easy to find locations for the howitzers. They could be moved almost anywhere. But as the ground softened and the rains came, the rice patties became a friend of the enemy and no friend of the artillery. We found ourselves located in hilly country, with valleys or cuts as the location of choice. Moving became a way of life, and operating out of the FDC truck provided a new set of problems. This was a small space without much ventilation. With lights out at night, and blackout conditions set, it became a real challenge to operate in the warmer weather.

The infantry was in the process of setting up a stable front. Our role was to assist them in the process. The FOs would pick targets of Chinese and North Korean assembly areas and we would fire to keep them dispersed, to prevent the formation of groups that could be used in a charge. The targets were usually village buildings, road crossings, holes, and caves. Movement generally happened at night. Whenever the FOs heard or saw movement, they would alert our gun crews. Naturally the gun crews would cuss because they were losing sleep, but they always accepted the challenge. There was a great amount of activity daily. We fired hundreds of shells in their direction—more work for me because I was then in charge of filing the daily ammo report, a job usually done by the sergeant, who was trying his best to be transferred to Japan where he had a woman waiting for him.

When we advanced, the Chinese and North Koreans mined the roads as a means of slowing our advance. It was not unusual for the wire crews to encounter these mines when laying cables along the sides of the road or in the ditches. The two standard wire section vehicles were the three quarter-ton weapons carrier truck and the standard jeep. The truck could carry more wire and men, allowing the jeep to move into areas not easily accessible. Both vehicles were equipped with a tripod arrangement that supported the roles of wire that unreeled as the truck went along the roads. The wire-crew members walked behind the trucks and in the ditches. Occasionally a truck or jeep ran over the mines and was destroyed. In other cases the mines injured or killed wire crews as they walked. Sometimes the mines got both.

At this time the order came down that all troops must wear their helmets. All winter the regulation had not been enforced. Now, for some reason, because we were in an area where incoming rounds and infiltrators were possible, the brass decided that Tin Tops were mandatory. The order was not well received. All winter we had used the helmets as containers for water, for cooking or for heating "C" rations. Now we had to wear them. But the order included all officers and so we begrudgingly accepted. After all, an order was an order.

By the third of April we were three miles from the 38th parallel, firing across the line. The 27th moved very fast under our fire.

For the first time, our FDC was located within active mortar range. Although the enemy had artillery, they used small arms, mortars and hand grenades to good advantage. Also, propaganda leaflets were shot at us in mortar shells. The paper they used was poor, yellowed stock. Much of the printing was blurred. The leaflets contained propaganda statements about how futile our situation was and how they would offer good treatment to us if we threw down our arms. We laughed, as they must have done whenever we fired our propaganda leaflets at them.

One of the first things the FOs did every morning or evening, when he and his jeep/radio unit was in place, was to turn on his radio and check in with FDC. Our radio would come to life with "Fandango 3, this is FO Able. Are you up and ready? Over."

If I was in operation at the time, my response would be "Fandango 3. We copy you, Able. What's up? Over."

His response: "Mark prep fire number 1. All batteries."

I would respond: "Roger, stand by for round one."

With that information I would alert the batteries to stand by for a fire mission and send the prearranged data for target, prep fire, number 1. One round.

When I received the statement "On the way, Able battery," I would relay this to the FO. "Able battery on the way, one round. Over."

We would then wait for his acknowledgement of "on target," or make adjustments as he ordered. If adjustments were required we would notify the battery. This would then be repeated for the other two batteries.

The FO might request more prep targets. It was an individual thing depending on their location in proximity to the enemy forces.

If they were in a static position and there was wire to the FO, the checking in would be done by telephone. The answer to the ring would be "Lightning 3. Sergeant Holmsten, here."

Telephone was much easier, but radio was used most often. We never used or knew the name of the FO person. It was always FO Able for the one attached to A Company, and FO Baker for the one attached to B Battery and FO Charlie for the one attached to C Battery. After a while we would work out catch terms to identify people. "Is that you, Tex?" was an example. Buckwheat was another. Brig was used for the one we considered to be the best FO. He got the position after being released from the guardhouse in Fort Lewis, Washington, in exchange for volunteering for combat duty in Korea. I met him only once. He had managed to stay alive and well and remained to the end our best and most effective Forward Observer.

Combat fatigue took its toll as much as actual fighting. Men worried, cried, hated, cursed, thought the entire world was against them, fought with their conscience and the turmoil back home, raged at their inability to help their loved ones through moments of trial. Sickness, the smell, the punishing routines, the dirt and mud, the unclean conditions and the snapping officers, often caused men to break.

Never was combat fatigue brought home as clearly as it was one day when I and another guy were sitting on our helmets eating a meal. "Smitty" was from a southern state. I can't remember which one. He was a slight lad, with dark hair, thin-faced, a kid who wore his sorrow like a mask. It was hard sometimes to get words out of him. He always seemed somewhere else, back home perhaps, concentrating on something other than war. That day, when we were eating, he suddenly stopped, laid down his mess kit, looked into the sky, pulled his .45 automatic out of his holster and pointed it at his knee.

He grumbled something, then fired a round.

Smitty toppled to the ground without a whimper, held his leg in pain, writhed like a madman. I can't remember all I did. I shouted, leaned down, rolled him over on his back, clamped my hands around his thigh. He didn't bleed much. His eyes were glazed, sightless it seemed. Words mumbled at his lips amid the saliva. Medics came running. They took him away. I couldn't finish my meal. I remember walking away, perhaps in circles, my hands trembling. How could things ever get that bad, I thought, that a man would shoot himself? Yet, they did. It was not the first time or the last.

Another time, a man from the wire/radio section got angry with the communications officer and the major. He started shooting randomly at their tents. He was tackled by others, taken down, was hauled away. I never knew what happened to him—ended up in a guardhouse somewhere, I suppose. It could only be explained as combat fatigue.

It also brought out the hatred in men. One of the corporals, who had accompanied the S-2 on recon patrols when they first arrived in Korea, harbored a grudge that came to life one night as we were sitting around a fire. He always blamed the S-2 for the time they had nearly been killed in an ambush situation. His hatred burst one night, perhaps because he had been drinking, perhaps because he couldn't hold the anger any longer, perhaps because he was fed up with the entire war, the danger, the fear. Out of the blue, he looked the S-2 in the eye and with a sneer on his lips, he told him that the next time they went on patrol, he wasn't coming back.

We were shocked. The S-2 was unmoved. The corporal just stared him down. The S-2 stood up, walked away. Soon two MPs came and tied the corporal's wrists behind his back, led him off. The corporal never said a word. His eyes said everything. We never saw him again. He went back to Service Battery, from there to a brig or to a hospital. Combat fatigue? It was anyone's guess. People snapped for no reason. Calm one minute, flaming the next. It was the way of war, to spoil one's soul, to take a good man and turn him foul, like the rice paddies in spring.

On April 5, General Ridgeway ordered a new advance toward an objective line called Kansas. Operation Rugged, as it was named, was approximately 115 miles in length, including the 14 miles of muddy tidal water on the left flank and the ten-mile water barrier of the Hwach'on Reservoir in the center. Kansas would become a base for larger operations designed to seize the Iron Triangle. Our role was in close support to the 27th.

I was angry for a time. A former supply sergeant who had been in FDC, who had transferred out because he didn't like the job, was coming back into our section and it was up to us to teach him. The assistant supply corporal, an RA, was making sergeant. It seemed unfair that they should make rates, when we worked so hard and got nowhere. I thought for a time that I might put in for transfer to a firing battery or a gun section. I also thought they had bypassed my OCS application in favor of regular army applications. I was peeved.

147

I thought hard work and dedication to duty had little to do with promotions.

As to the 38th parallel, we were firing over it daily but did not cross with any force. We were busy shelling the Chinese, to keep our boys from suffering major losses.

We lost two men ourselves during that period. A boy in "B" Battery was run over by a two and a half ton truck while he slept on the ground, crushed his head. Luckily the ground was soft, pressed him into it, kept him from being killed. The doc said he would survive. Another sergeant jumped to catch a football, came down on a rock. He broke his ankle. Damndest thing.

Worked a full eight-hour shift and a two and a half-hour night shift. Little time for myself. Most of the off time is taken up by moving.

On April 7 we received word that we were going into reserve, that the 27th combat team would move back below Seoul for a rest. The Turks were in the process of relieving our boys. In preparation for the pullout we fired at all the hot spots to keep the Chinese in their holes.

I looked forward to a little rest and relaxation, away from the hectic routine. We got a football from Special Services, either through a request or simply by accident. I was interested in playing and I immediately began organizing a touch football game for diversion and exercise. I got about ten guys involved. It wasn't real football, not as I remembered it in high school or college. Mostly it was yelling and shouting, scuffing and pushing, no real strategy. Passes were wobbly. Runs were seldom effective. Missed calls. Dropped balls. We played in combat boots. Our helmets were placed on the sidelines with our rifles stacked. The captain didn't like the idea of football. There was always a chance of a twisted ankle, a broken leg or some other injury that might put someone out of action. But he allowed it, even though we were "on line" and not in "reserve." He knew that if a fire mission was called or if a march order came, we'd scramble. It was good fun, except for the aches and pains that came the next day. The USO was rumored to be coming up with some kind of show, Hollywood celebrities, singers, dancers, girls. We hoped they would come our way.

KOREAN LAUNDRY. Whenever we were near an open river the locals hustled every Army unit close by for the opportunity to make a few cents and do laundry. The flowing river with the rock pounding treatment was the cleaning process used.

One of the old Mama-sans took my dirty clothes and washed them in a stream. It was not unusual for them to wash GI clothes for an entire day on their knees. They soaked the clothes, then scrubbed them with soap, pounded them clean on a flat rock and hung them up to dry. The clothes always came back clean from those rudimentary laundries.

We received our first draftee replacements on the 6th of April, men plucked from civilian life just as we were, and all young kids. In the group was Bob Baur, Ron Scheffer and a guy from the South, a married man with a family. He was bitter. I don't recall his name. Ron was a graduate from an Ivy League college in Massachusetts and an All-American goaltender for the college soccer team. He was well trained. He fitted in fast. Bob Baur was a trained radioman assigned to the FDC. He learned real fast and was a good addition.

He was from Lansing, Michigan, and had worked in the Oldsmobile factory. He was an auto expert. Sefton latched on to him like milk to cornflakes. They made a good team. Bob Schranck was away when the three men arrived. We were glad to get three above-average, intelligent replacements.

The new guys got a good baptism of fire. The Chinese came down while we worked the entire night shift on fire missions. They attacked at night, with blowing bugles and swarms of men. Pure numbers and noise. It would go from a dead quiet to a great commotion in a matter of minutes. Their method was to get the U.S. soldiers in a state of panic. When this occurred, the 155 howitzers in the rear would throw up very bright parachute flares so the FOs could see what was happening. If the weather was good the flares would light up the entire sky. We had timed rounds that would burst above the advancing infantry. After the Chinese charge it was always expected that we would move, forward if we were successful, back if they were successful. Move and kill. Kill and move. A vicious cycle that went on and on and on. On that particular night we stopped them. And color returned to the faces of the three new men.

The next day I hiked over to the shower unit for the first time in a week and washed away my Korean Krud. We were fortunate to have the showers so close.

The weather was warm now, about 60 degrees, balmy but heavy with the stench of the rice paddies. The nights were still cool, sometimes a 20 degree drop, enough to use the feather bag. Sleeping on a cot was preferred but it was much harder to stay warm. The cold came up from underneath, making it uncomfortable, even though we were living in a tent. Sometimes a straw mat was better than a cot.

The Turks hadn't moved out yet but the relief was complete. They were almost in the Ingin River, the high spot on the front. They would wait for the line to straighten before moving forward. They always seemed to get the job of holding the line at some point. Then they pushed. It was a tactic they used effectively. Seldom did the Chinese get the upper hand on the Turks.

They showed a movie in the morning, *Harvey* with James Stewart. It took all morning to show a two-hour film because the power went off and on.

I went to the medic in the afternoon and played canasta with the doctor. Even they had their idle times. When the wounded came, they came in droves. Mass confusion. Then it would quiet down and the cards would come out. The M.A.S.H. boys were a great bunch. Lots of fun.

On the 10th, we again commenced firing across the 38th parallel. At times the outlook of the war seemed bright. At other times it seemed bleak. Death was always on patrol.

Quiet at night. Stars out in abundance, like gems on black velvet. The smell was gone. The wind brought the scent of new growth, the wetness of the earth. Sefton and I sat on the hillside looking south across the ragged ridge to where the valley fell away to mother its only stream. He smoked. We both got to talking about how the RA enlisted men and officers were the preferred soldiers. It was a favorite topic of his. Then he strayed back to home, to where his mind was. He said he would have started his third year at Brown the coming fall and that he had received another package of bread from his Dad.

I knew what that meant. His father always packed a bottle of Scotch inside the hollowed loaf for mailing protection. He invited me to have a nightcap later on.

He blew a string of smoke out in front of him, watched it disappear in the wind, asked me if I wanted to read any of his new books. I told him I used my spare time to write letters. He told me I was henpecked already.

Sefton flipped his cigarette away into the darkness, a spiral of sparks. He said they were getting up a baseball team. He asked if I wanted to play. I said I would. Anything for diversion.

The night was brittle, the cold coming in. A drone in the sky behind us. We thought it was Bedcheck Charlie.

On April 11 the battle line was one and a half miles north of the 38th parallel. On that day our good friend, Bob Schranck, was assigned as an FO working with the 2nd Battalion of the 27th Infantry Regiment. The location was Kura Kura, Korea. On that day, Bob was wounded. He was sent to a MASH unit and then to a hospital in Japan. It was the first time one of our close buddies was hit. It saddened us all. We were now one man short in FDC.

We were shocked on April 11 to hear that President Truman had relieved General MacArthur of his command and replaced him with General Ridgeway. Aside from the political impact, we were glad to hear that MacArthur was out. General Ridgeway was a soldier's soldier, always for the troops. We took it as a good sign.

The closest we ever came to MacArthur was seeing his *Constellation* fly over one day on its way to Seoul. Other than that, he was an invisible leader. One thing Ridgeway did immediately was to round up all the surplus cooks in the service battery and send them forward. He ordered them to join the artillery headquarters and gun batteries and provide at least one hot meal a day to the line troops. The cooks just about panicked but they came forward with their field kitchens and we got hot meals, including eggs fried to order. The kitchen crew became good friends of the FDC because we were on odd hours and thankful for whatever they could rustle up for us. One of the cooks was a well-fed veteran of World War II, who told stories about Audie Murphy, the Medal of Honor winner. He had cooked for him. His story was that Murphy went looking for trouble and was always out in front as a matter of thrill seeking. As for General Ridgeway, he came by occasionally to check on us. It was always inspiring to see him.

One of the problems with the FDC truck body was that it was small. In the past, FDC was the official information bureau, where one could find out what was going on, a place to escape the eyes of the CO. In the new truck, we didn't have room for slackers and the lieutenant was always there to incite conversations that were not always complimentary. One night he came into the truck when Sefton and I had duty. He sat down and started out with his usual banter, started railing me about continually writing letters home and not concentrating on my work. I tried hard to conceal my anger, told him I was preparing to go home. His voice remained caustic, reminding me that it would be a while before rotation caught up with me. He said if I was that important, the civilians would wait for me. I couldn't resist telling him that it was a good thing he was Regular Army. He'd starve to death in civilian life.

He bragged that he had it made in the Army. I shot back my standard remark, that if it weren't for his commission in the big war, he'd be out of here. I knew he was passed over for captain. The fact that he was an S-2 intelligence officer was the Army's way of keeping him out of FDC. Sefton agreed.

He reminded us that we were two of a kind, no brains and no respect for our officers. He said if he wasn't such a nice guy, he'd have us both up for insubordination. He also suggested that I keep my mouth closed.

I guess I received my bully training from my mother, when I was at a young age. One day I came into the house crying. I said a boy had just knocked me down. She didn't feel sorry for me at all, just stood in front of me and said, "You get back out there and show him that you won't back away from anything. You stand up to that bully." I carried that advice with me, to that day and beyond. I learned to be a fighter, not a wimp. To me, the lieutenant was just another bully.

We could talk like that to the lieutenant simply because we both knew Captain Joe couldn't stand him either. We also knew that if the captain went to the "old man," the commanding officer, Major Karl, he would only dismiss the matter. Bad Ass S-2 wouldn't get any sympathy from the higher brass. They knew that the real problem was Bad Ass himself.

We were still in support of the Turks but we also had three new men to break in. It was quiet on line. I read my mail several times over.

Our unit was starting to lose men to rotation. I estimated that my time would be up in August. So far we had lost seven men. The chief of section, SFC, was among the next group to go. We were glad to see his name on the list. I had hoped my rotation would get me home in time for Florence's graduation from college but that did not appear likely.

A few cases of yellow jaundice were reported. We started to receive malaria pills, part of our daily diet until first frost. No cases of typhoid or tetanus. The numerous shots we received must have paid off.

I wrote to the folks back home, asked them to send canned goods that could be used without a lot of cooking. We had a surplus of fruit cocktail. I craved fresh water from Minnesota. Ours was heavily chlorinated, for obvious reasons.

On April 17 we moved a long way. Dust rose in thick clouds from the dry roadbeds. We planted our guns along the east boundary of the 25th division, amid a collection of low hills. We were in what remained of Unchon-ni, on the main north-south road. The town was rubble. Nothing was useable. The weather was 60 degrees, no rain. I was assigned to the quiet shift, from 03:00 to 06:00.

With our move came a pleasant surprise: air mattresses. I was fortunate enough to get one. Scheffer also acquired a pup tent. Now we were by ourselves. I slept until 10:00, got up, shaved and had my hair cut. While my hair was being trimmed, the barber discovered that I had a slight case of impetigo. I went to the medic, got a salve from Doc Rubin to clear up the crud, as it was called. It was a scalp rash, acquired from not washing my hair often enough, further complicated by wearing a helmet.

We received a new battalion commander, whose job it was to locate positions for the headquarters company and all the gun batteries. He was convinced that headquarters battery should be in front of the gun batteries to shorten the wire connections. This meant another move. We ended up two miles from the front. Less wire. More danger. We moved in the rain, settled into position about 16:00. It was dark before we were operational. Despite our close proximity to the front, we didn't have much action. We were north of the river, in a quiet spot. But despite the serenity, the pace was hectic. We were constantly busy.

Looking at my 1:25,000 meters situation map, I found that we were 60,000 meters east (37.3 miles) and 20,000 meters north (12.4 miles) of the city of Kaesong in the village of Oji-Ni. The troops were drawing up a line that went diagonal across the peninsula starting at the Imgin River, going northwest almost on a straight line to the east coast. On the west we were still below the 38th parallel. Ever since we shifted to the right, through Pochan and Chunchon, we had been east of Seoul. We hadn't seen a town with a name for a long time. Towns were generally off-limits for troops due to disease and destruction. The Chinese had also been known to mine the towns. They were dangerous places.

We didn't have a good day on April 16. The Chinese decided to fight back and we really poured out the lead. Luckily, we and the infantry turned back the attack. The 27th lost about 30 men but they made it out okay. The gun crews were busy until 16:00, when I got my first break.

Gil, a medic working in the forward aid station, wanted someone to ride along with him to transport three wounded GIs and a wounded Chinese prisoner back to the M.A.S.H. unit in the rear. I was given the job of riding along so I could bring the ambulance back. The Chinese soldier was dressed in a normal gray, dirty uniform, if you could call it that. They lived in their clothes and off the land, except for the rice bag they carried. I don't recall how badly he was wounded. He didn't move during the entire ride. Doc Rubin helped him off the truck, along with the three other Americans, one who had died en route.

When I returned to FDC, we fired approximately 1,500 rounds to thwart another Chinese drive. We received a commendation from the general on the fine support. We really appreciated the pat on the back.

The Chinese continued to hit us hard. They struck at 03:00, had everyone on their feet, ready to roll should the 27th fold under pressure. We fired nonstop. Both flanks were hit hard. The FDC and gun batteries were split so that one gun battery could cover our move. In cases like that, the FO dealt directly with the gun battery, hoping for the best. We moved a little south to a new position. The line formed in front of us. The Chinese occupied the spot we had just vacated.

Another long night. The entire headquarters battery pulled back except for a few of us in FDC. It was our second position in one night, moving in the dark, guns and trucks, going in a seemingly aimless direction away from the sound of battle. Setting up. Firing. No sleep. Tired and dragging, we moved with the bending line. It appeared as though the 24th Infantry Regiment had taken the brunt of the charge. Their line had broken. Whenever the Chinese got an open spot they poured all they could through the hole. We were in danger for a while. I believe it was the 27th who stemmed the tide.

Infantry and tanks were dug in right around our position. We waited for the 24th to pull back. There was battle noise in front of us. I hoped the momentum would shift, so we wouldn't have to move again.

The 6th ROK broke again but the British boys held tight. There were rumors that the 40th Division was coming from Japan to fill the 6th ROK hole. But would they come in time? Every minute was important. In one spot the Chinese poured two battalions through a hole, made a big gap in the line. The 35th Infantry Regiment folded under the onslaught. We had to move again.

With the battle at our backs, we moved south once more, found another position, fired again and again, and again. Many targets. Many rounds. Sleep, like the war, went unattended. Were it not for the constant rush of adrenaline, the fear, the driving force to succeed, I would have fallen asleep on the plot board. But we kept going, hour after hour, until the Chinese were eventually held at bay. With the grind of battle at a virtual standstill for a few hours, I crawled into my pup tent and collapsed, until I was rousted out to move again.

We moved for the fourth time on the 24th, with two of the gun batteries. All of headquarters battery and one gun battery were sent back to occupy a blocking position to protect us from being cut off. It was 06:00 when one of our crews went back up again, to fire for retreat.

We found ourselves southwest of Chongson-a-san, on the main road. We were lucky. Not one of our men had been hurt during the moves. I sacked out after the sun rose, but was up again at noon when we moved once more, south of the town. It was fairly quiet there. We fired only a few rounds. I realized then, in the relative silence, how close we had come to being overrun. It left a choking feeling in my throat, especially when I heard that the Chinese infantry had wiped out an entire medical collecting station, killing the doctors, patients and aid men. I prayed to God that I wouldn't have to experience another night like that.

But the next night was the same. The Chinese broke through "G" Company with about 2,000 men. We proceeded to pour about 1,900 rounds into the area. Then the reserve company rushed in and stabilized the line. We had a lot of enemy between us and the infantry, so we had to sweat out another night and wait for the morning sun to determine the damage. I was up and working until 03:30. It was a long night. But it was better to be up than sweat out the attack in my bag. At least when I was working, I was contributing. Fear always reached razor edge when the Chinese got within gun range. Then we'd have to move again and fast.

I slept the next day, amid relative calm. Once again the line had stabilized.

April 27th: quiet. The spring rains had officially started. Muddy again. The Koreans were planting their rice paddies. The sky was gunmetal gray, a slick, wet color all the way to the horizon. Planes overhead were heard but not seen. I slept well for about eight hours. Awoke to a slight drizzle. Ate rations inside my tent.

Moved again in the afternoon. Headquarters battery on the road back to Yong-Dong-Po. We were eating with the battery, better chow, hot food for a change.

We were now at a point where we could hit the enemy right between the eyes. Our losses had not been great when compared with those of the enemy. There must have been thousands of Chinese dead on the hillsides. Our boys always pulled back rather than face them in hand-to-hand combat and let the artillery level them. They had thousands to send against us. The only way to even the odds is to kill as many as possible when they sound their bugles. So we would pull back and give it to them.

Had a grand total of three hours sleep until we moved again. We spent most of the day moving, reached our position about 15:00. I waited for supper, which was about 16:00 and then hit the sack. I slept ten hours. We were in a house again, out of the rain, in a room 6 × 12, eight men side by side. Another of the rooms held 20 men, officers and enlisted. Cozy living. At least we were dry.

At breakfast the next morning we talked about rotation again. Thus far, since rotation had started on the 10th, 45 men had gone home. There were 383 men in the first category with six months' duty. It appeared that it would be a long time before I was eligible. At that point all I could hope for was to be home by my first anniversary. That would have given me nine months in Korea. If I wasn't buggy by then, I would be awful close. I toyed with the idea of putting in for R&R, a seven-day relief trip to Japan even though it would lose points. I would liked to have gone with Bob Schranck, but he wasn't back from the hospital.

We talked about where the war was heading, having given up some ground to the enemy. Until then we had been very lucky. We could only hope that the line would hold and that we could begin pushing north again. As it was, we could only wait for them to make their move.

They always hit us at night, when they couldn't be seen.

13

BASEBALL, BUGS, AND WHITE GIRLS

A quiet May 1st. Warm day. Clouds like white brushstrokes against the blue sky. I heard a bird singing. Music coming from one of the tents, a peppy song that lifted my spirits. No rain, just a fresh breeze carrying a scent I couldn't identify. A soldier working on a truck was whistling. New sounds on the edge of the calm.

Later we would send out an armored task force, light tanks or half-tracks in place of our usual recon vehicles. We wanted to know what's out there, to locate the enemy. The same thing happened before when we pushed north. It appeared we might be making a move again.

We lost nine men to rotation, one from St. Paul who was a friend of mine, John, from Washington High School. I was surprised to find his name on the list. I never knew he was there.

We finished sandbagging the FDC truck. We got a bulldozer from the engineers to flatten the area and dig out a wall for protection. The truck was protected on three sides.

In the afternoon, when it was hot, I went to the Han-Chon-Se River, 6,000 yards east and 3,000 yards north of where it joined with the Han. I stripped down to my skivvies and waded out into the cold water, washed down, laid for a while on the bank where the grass was beginning to grow. Had the sun on my face. For a while it reminded me of a day at Lake Josephine. The only thing missing was the chatter, the laughter, the splashing of those in the water, the remarkably wonderful sounds of a beach filled with kids. It was one of those few halcyon moments one carved out of the war, a brief interlude of peace, a reminder of how the world would be if it weren't so filled with hate.

Upon returning to camp, I learned we were losing three men out of FDC. One of the three didn't fit in. Another went to the motor pool as a mechanic, the third to outpost guard detail. That meant we would go back to full eight-hour shifts every day, and three hours at night, until we received some more replacements. Got the *Stars and Stripes* about five days late, learned a bit more about MacArthur's removal. We didn't get much through AFRS (Armed Forces Radio Station). They played music most of the time, interspersed with a few broadcasts from the States. They didn't broadcast much political news that might rile up the troops.

We did some firing during the day, some prearranged firing at night. Another tank/infantry team went out, came back with 22 prisoners and an estimated 200 bodies of the enemy. We were biding our time, waiting for something to happen. I worked from noon to 16:00. It was payday. I drew out $10. I now had $261 in a fund that would probably grow to about $500 when I was rotated. Not a lot, but a start on civilian life again.

Rained again, hard. That night two men came into the truck while I was working, carrying their soaking wet sleeping bags, said they needed a spot to sleep.

I refused them, told them to take their bags someplace else, that this was an FDC truck, not a bunkhouse. I suggested they go over to the wire section, or to the medic tent. When they complained, I told them the brass would chew me out if any unauthorized people entered the vehicle. They grumbled, yanked out their bag, gave me a familiar swear word and went back into the rain.

The rain was always a problem. When we sandbagged the truck we made a dam across the small cut in front of the truck. When it rained, the water flowed down the creek bed and dammed up behind the sandbags until it ran around the dammed area. Stallard and another guy had pitched their tent on a high spot next to the truck where they appeared to be high and dry. When it rained, the water backed up until they were sleeping in water. Stallard showed up with his bag and offered to go to work. How could I refuse Stallard? His buddy was still sleeping in the wet bag.

When it rained there wasn't much to do. I stayed out of the weather and in my pup tent. Scheffer and I got up at noon, ate lunch,

RIVER IN KOREA. One hot afternoon I found myself resting on a rock in a flowing river and one of my buddies snapped this picture. Relaxing was a rare event and always enjoyed.

worked until 16:00 and stayed past my shift to wait for chow. Then I accepted an invitation to play pinochle with the medics in their warm, dry tent. I enjoyed being with the medics. Doc Rubin was Jewish. Oliver was Negro. Joe Quartararo was Italian. We were all soldiers with no race, color or religious distinction at all. Just GIs. We had a good time. Lots of laughs. Being with them was the best thing about the Army, the camaraderie, the common goal, the deep-seated loyalty, man for man, to stay alive, to go home.

Summer came like the lifting of a shade. It was 70 degrees on May 6. The sun was sizzling once again, the air dusty from the hills. The groundwater had all dried up, hardening the mud. A gray haze hung over the roads. We were still in the same spot, hadn't fired a single round for a few days. It appeared we were waiting for the Chinese to hit. We are the main defense for Seoul. We thought they might come our way.

Scheffer and I took a bath in a small stream that flowed past the tent. Under the right conditions and with a few trees above us, it would have been ideal spot. The little creek came with the rains. It was fed by a flowing spring, high enough up so we could catch the water and divert it with ammo boxes, elevated enough to create a waterfall, thus a crude shower. Another feat of basic GI engineering.

The supply truck came by later on, clunking and rattling. It was hung with every kind of utensil, bag, gun, uniform, cot, tent, bucket or box available to the Army. It looked more like a traveling sideshow than a supply truck. One would think it was a huckster coming to sell his wares. He had everything except patent medicine or booze. And probably some of that was hidden away behind or beneath all the other gear. He had new fatigues, the ones with new nylon thread that glistened in the sun. I tried on a pair size 36. They were a bit too tight. I was one of his problem fits. He forgot to bring the special issue socks I had asked for. He said he would send them up special delivery. I got a can of pineapple, a few sheets of writing paper, and a new pen to replace the one I had jammed into the plotboard when arguing with the S-2.

I found out I would be the second man in our outfit to go home once they started rotation on the enlisted reserves. Most of them that had arrived in October and November went into the infantry. I was lucky, all around.

I also learned that the Chinese were less than 1,000 yards on both sides of us when we pulled out that first morning four months earlier. The infantry in front of us took a heavy shelling. Our forward guns got in a few rounds even as they took a pounding from the Chinese mortars. We fell back. They guarded our retreat. The 155 FA Battalion that backed the 19th Infantry Regiment lost 158 men and 11 guns because they were overrun. Good men lost. When reports like that came in, I hated the war to an even greater degree. Hate and sorrow and fear and death. The battlefield was full of it.

I received mail from home, cookies, canned goods, envelopes, and razor blades.

Charlie Battery called in the afternoon, wanted to play ball. We accepted. A fellow in the wire section got the guys together. I was excused from my regular shift so I could play. We carved out a field on a flat piece of land, buried pieces of an old ammunition box for plates, set up a canvas for a backstop. We had a terrific time. It was our first outing and even though we didn't do well, our team had promise. I caught, got a couple of hits. It was fun to play with the battery boys. Even though I was stiff and sore after the game, I knew my legs, arms and body would adjust to exercise quickly. With the help of the officers, I would play again. It was a good diamond. It felt good to play ball again. Made me almost forget where I was.

The *Stars and Stripes* indicated that all enlisted reserves would fit into rotation as soon as their names and points qualified them, without any regard to serial number. That made regular army and enlisted reserves equal in points and rotation spots. Good news for all concerned.

Weather was hot again. Sunburn was beginning to take its toll on some of the guys. I was lucky in that I tanned quickly, didn't burn. Some of the guys got red as a beet, had to cover up. It was rough on them when we had division inspection.

I was busy all day on the 11th. At breakfast two fellows from "C" company came over and told me they were going to play the 2nd Battalion of the 27th Infantry Regiment. They asked me if I'd like to catch for them. They got me all fired up. Our CO arranged the game so I had no problem getting approval to leave the area.

A fellow from "A" battery pitched. The regular catcher from "C" battery started as catcher. I went in after a few innings. We won 4 to 2. It was a well-played game. The GI spectators got a real kick out of watching. They were a loud and boisterous cheering section. They had bet $600, so there was incentive to shout. It was a new experience to see spectators lining both sides of the field, each holding a loaded gun. Made one not want to make a mistake.

Got back about noon, found out that our CO had watched the game. He was pleased with the outcome. He assured me that I would play again.

In the afternoon I went down to the creek again and soaked in the cool water. Laid in the sun. Drowsed away the lazy afternoon. That night I got a good night's sleep. What luxury.

The next day we started area drill schedules, inspections, all the usual garrison duties. It was much like the old "chicken army" with

163

the officers showing off their power. They generally didn't like enlisted reserves, and they displayed their dislike like the shine on their bars.

Weather was warm. Bugs started to appear. Mosquito bars were issued. Ah, yes, mosquito bars. The army's bug protection devices. They consisted of mosquito netting sewn to completely cover a one-man pup tent or a cot. Once this was pulled over a tent it was a struggle to crawl in and seal off the openings against mosquitoes. In addition to the netting, we were also issued bug spray to use inside the tent, in case the mosquito bars didn't work.

When the Chinese started using artillery we didn't use big tents because they attracted attention. Scheffer and I were tenting together. We were on the same schedule, night and day. He was engaged to be married as soon as he returned home. His girlfriend was a bacteriologist who worked on whooping cough serum in a Boston research lab.

I was contacted by a fellow in "B" Battery and asked to catch for them against "F" Company, 27th Infantry. My reputation as a good catcher was spreading. "B" Battery had a good team. A big Indian from Texas was their pitcher. He had an excellent fastball. Unfortunately, we lost 5 to 4 in eight innings. After it was over, I boasted being a catcher for three different teams, "C," "B," and Headquarters Battery. Scuttlebutt had it that if "C" and "B" Batteries merged they would represent the battalion. More fun. Less war.

May 13 was Mother's Day. The chaplain held a church service. We sat on our helmets with our rifles across our legs. The service was different, moving. I prayed for my mother. I thanked God for all the days she had given me, for her guidance in both material and spiritual matters. I appreciated more and more the things she had done for me, for they had helped me face my daily tasks in the army. I missed the dinners at the Curtis Hotel, the afternoon rides, the church services. It brought me back to perfect times. The chaplain spoke from 2nd Timothy. It was a wonderful, inspiring service. The Spirit of God was with me, there, on that desolate stretch of Korean countryside.

We were still in a stagnant position and I was content to remain that way. We suspected the enemy would hit us in the East, not on our perimeter. We had settled into routine garrison duty, which was nothing more than a planned time killer. We had a half hour each morning of hup-two-three-four, then classes of every variety to review things we already knew. Even though it was boring at times, it was better than the constant move, fire, move routine we had been on during the preceding several months.

The following day I was in the medics' tent, using their stationary, staying dry out of the hard, steady rain. A dreary day. Drill sessions in the morning. Sat around and talked with Smiley and Tim until noon, saying goodbye. They both left that afternoon for the States.

I slept most of the afternoon, expecting to have the 03:30 to 06:00 shift, only to find out I had the night off. Schef and I made supper on our small stove, heated a can of beans, opened a can of cake. After supper, we both went to the medics and played cards. Schef and I got beat in a game of pinochle. We crawled into our tents late. It was still raining. A constant rapping on our tents but not enough to keep me awake.

We hadn't fired a round all that week. The rain was our only enemy.

My tent was high and dry when the rain stopped. We had good ditches around our tent so the water could drain off. Others were not quite as lucky. Several of the boys were swamped. I got up about 11:00 only to learn that I was assigned to a MG (machine gun) crew for the purposes of test firing. Division Artillery was coming and we were instructed to demonstrate that we knew how to fire the weapons. I hoped I could show them what they wanted to see. I knew only how to feed the ammunition and pull the trigger. Beyond that, I was a novice. But we did all right. By the time our demonstration was over, I had a good idea of how to operate a machine gun.

Our section received booster shots. I got all three in my arm: typhoid, cholera and Jap B. The typhoid was the roughest. Sore arm for two days. The Jap B was a series of three shots, one week apart. The Jap B protected against an infected bee sting that was 85 percent fatal without the shots. With that kind of odds, we lined up eagerly for the needle.

After the shots we rebuilt some of the sandbags around the FDC truck, dug a new channel to carry the water away. The 16th was a quiet day. Almost everyone was gone except Stallard and me. Our three sergeants took off for the forward observation post to practice being FOs. They had accepted the voluntary mission as a means for fast advancement. Two of them were up for commissions.

I made new grid sheets during the afternoon hours while some of the new men went to classes on the machine gun.

Bob Schranck was still on the missing list. I wondered why he hadn't written.

Had the night off. Got a good night's sleep. Scuttlebutt indicated that our quiet period was about to end: the Chinese were stirring.

By 04:30 the situation had indeed changed. The Chinese made a big push against the east front and hit us hard. As I was working, a whole list of reports came in and we commenced firing. The Turks were out in front of us, confronting a surge of Chinese infantry. We dusted off our guns to the tune of about 700 rounds. We got a report that we really helped turn back the attack. We had helped the cause. If the line held, we would move north again.

Every time the telephone rang we always had a new fire mission. The Chinese had turned north, so I hoped we would get some peace and quiet again. The line, for the moment, was silent.

We worked the next day repairing a washed out wall around the FDC truck, used many new sandbags to re-route the streambed. We also strung barbed wire for protection, even though we knew the wire would not stop anyone. The major ordered it, so the wire was strung. We had a very good outpost security system but now we had barbwire separating the Headquarters Battery from the firing batteries. We were not happy campers.

The new fellows that had arrived the month before were becoming involved in routine accidents with firearms. One medic put an unintentional hole in the roof of the ambulance. A kid in the wire section built a fire over some live ammo crates and got nicked between his legs.

By the 20th, the push north had started. We knew we'd be ordered up.

I awoke to the sound of stateside music. I stuck my head out of the tent, saw Schef standing there buttoning his shirt. I asked him what was up. His face lit up like a boy ready to go to a dance. He said there were women over by the medic tent, that the USO had sent them up in a Special Services truck. They were handing out donuts and coffee. I came right out of my sack.

Over by the medic tent, the boys were lined up ten deep. Sure enough. The girls were there, all dressed up in low-buttoned white blouses and brightly colored aprons. They all wore a big smile. Most were shapely, hourglass types, the kind we called Petty girls. They spooned out as much merriment as they did donuts, laughing, winking, cavorting, to energize the men. Blondes, brunettes, a redhead. Something for everyone. They didn't put on an actual show. They were there to tell us that the home folks cared for us. Cat calls ensued. The girls ate up the attention. The men devoured their beauty. Donuts and coffee were secondary. Just looking at a beautiful woman was enough to rally the men, like a bright ray of sunlight. The "White Girls" as they were called, stayed around for about two hours. Everyone enjoyed the change of pace. Most of the men ate more than one donut.

I was on duty later in the afternoon, to put down a Chinese thrust. Luckily, they turned and retreated, out of range. We settled back into routine, but only for a while. Later that day we moved again, from what had become a stable position. When we settled down we were within shouting distance of the Chinese.

It rained again. The ground turned to mud. We were close to the Wangseek-ch'on River, about seven miles north and eight miles east of Seoul, in a wooded area. Lots of bugs, pesky things that got in our ears and mouth, hung around our heads in swarms. Out came the spray cans, our artillery for insects. Nothing more annoying than bugs. We accused the Chinese of sending them over just to irritate us.

We moved again on the 23rd, back along the same route, ended up east of the small river, 33,000 meters, or 20.5 miles, south of the 38th parallel. We were behind the 24th Infantry Regiment.

We had late chow, then decided to show a movie. We were in a draw, which gave us a good spot in which to put up an outdoor screen. The movie was *Panic on the Street*, a thriller about a Navy doctor in New Orleans with a plague on his hands. Not a good show.

But it provided a break. The movie was over at 23:00. It didn't allow for much sleep before I went on duty watch at 04:00.

We moved again, followed the river north to a place called King's Forest. We were on its southeast corner. It was a beautiful place. A narrow river flowed right past our door. Across the stream was an irrigation ditch about knee deep with clean, cool water. A good place to take a bath. The weather was hot, dry. The heat carried right through into the night. We slept without our heavy bags. Rumor had it that we were going on a task force with the 27th RCT.

The replacement situation seemed stagnant. They expected Stallard and me to train our replacements but they did not give us the rank to go with the responsibility. To top it all off, they gave a sergeant, who came from supply to FDC, a commission as a 2nd lieutenant. Both Stallard and I had been offered the opportunity at one time but they seemed to have forgotten about it. Perhaps it was because of our unwillingness to become forward observers. I wanted out. They wanted a 90-day extension. My aspirations of being an officer went down with the setting sun.

I was gaining weight at a rapid rate, through inactivity. Even the ball games did not help shrink my waist. My 36-inch size pants were tight. A 42 was just below comfortable. I found myself somewhere in between sizes, depending on the meals we ate and the activity that was available. We were eating a lot of canned meat, dehydrated eggs, spuds. They couldn't keep fresh food, especially when we were on the move.

We moved again on the 24th. Moved again on the 25th. Raining again. They said we could look forward to two more days of rain. Then it will be a hot, dry week. But who could trust a weatherman? The weather blues continued to plague us.

On the 28th we found ourselves firing over the 38th parallel again. It rained all night and right into the morning of the move. We were in a extensive valley. The entire battalion was set up within the hills. It was impressive to see guns and trucks as far as my eyesight allowed, hundreds of them, hunkered down. A landing strip had been carved in the center of the valley, to be used by our spotter planes. Also in the valley were remnants of a vicious firefight that occurred when the 555 FA of the 24th Infantry Division and a group of tanks got trapped when the Chinese pushed through. Destroyed guns, burned-out tanks, and shattered trucks littered the area. The 555 FA lost 158 men that day along with 11 guns. It was evident that they had unhooked their howitzers and were firing point blank into the Chinese when they were over-run. After the battle, the Air Force came in and put all the equipment out of commission to prevent the Chinese from using it. Charred and twisted and blackened by napalm, it remained a grim reminder of the vicious battle. The 155th were on their third set of guns. They'd had it rough.

Our friends in the medics had split up. I hadn't seen them for about a week. When I did return to their tent, I learned that Mac had gone to Service Battery. Bask had gone home. The two new medics were wise guys. Our pinochle games were history.

Had a quiet day on the 29th. We were still in support of the 24th Infantry. They reported no activity. We didn't fire a round. We knew the lull would end because at 06:00 the 27th was going in again. Apparently there was something in the wind but we didn't know what it was.

That night I missed my dog tags. I looked all over, couldn't find them, remembered that I might have left them at the creek. I didn't need them on a daily basis but when rotation came around I wouldn't be able to leave my unit without a complete set. The following morning I went back to the creek before the laundry ladies arrived, and found them right where I'd left them.

We moved across the 38th parallel the next day, twice. I was up from midnight until about 03:30. We were in a task force on the road to Chorwon, which was a fairly large town in the middle of Korea about 18 miles north of the 38th, and 37 miles east of Kaesong.

When we moved into one of the empty houses we found a woman there, shot between the eyes. It was the first civilian corpse I had seen, murdered or executed. Perhaps this woman hadn't been able to give the Chinese food or she had failed to answer their questions. The dead woman was dressed in local peasant clothing. She was not a combatant. We lifted her out, laid her on the ground, called the burial detail. They took her body away. I was sick at heart. Being a 21-year-old American from Minnesota, I was not accustomed to seeing dead people with holes in their head, flies crawling on their faces, their bodies stiff with rigor mortis. Sometimes I wondered if the Chinese were human.

It came to mind then that I had only fired my weapon once, the day we were in retreat from Seoul. I hadn't fired it at a person but rather at several barrels of gasoline that I was told to destroy. At the time, the gun crews were burning all their powder bags. Everything was on fire. The colonel ordered me to shoot holes in the tanks, so I did. No one was ever in my gun sight, nor do I think I was ever in theirs. But after seeing the dead woman, it would have been much easier to shoot one of the enemy.

The weather had improved. That night I put up our mosquito bar, slept on top of my bag until the last hour toward morning.

We were in the clouds most of the time. They settled low in the valley like a damp fleece. I found an old horse collar and bones near the location of an abandoned Chinese artillery position.

Apparently, people weren't the only things the Chinese soldiers killed.

14

THE WAR
COMES CLOSER

June: that best of months. The oncoming summer, bright blue skies, freshness in the air. At least that was how I remembered the onset of June, as being ripe with new birth. But it wasn't that way on line, not in Korea, not when the Chinese had us in their sights.

We were supporting the advance units of the 27th Infantry that day. They were out in front of the main defensive line. The FDC truck was dug into a ravine, sandbagged all around, protected from everything except a direct hit. My tent was also sandbagged. I had dug a foxhole next to it for added protection, not knowing what would come, if anything, or when it would come, if ever. We planned for the worst, hoped for the best.

The incoming mortar rounds came with the dawn, awakening me with a start. The moment I heard the first WHOOSH, I knew instantly we were under attack. The terrible, frightening sound of the projectile carving through air brought me to instant alert. A second later I heard the explosion, a dull thump as the ground erupted. The canvas of my tent shivered. Another. That rippling sound of horror. Then another. Closer this time. I leaped out of my bag and grabbed my weapon, poked my head outside the tent.

More rounds came. Further out I saw the flashes, the smoke, the bursting earth, down near the ravine where Sefton and Ron Scheffer were tented. The medics ran past, two of them, carrying a stretcher, headed toward the ravine where a spool of smoke took shape.

I dove into my foxhole, crouched down behind the sandbags, heard small arms fire far out, cackling, muffled, like popcorn going

SANDBAGGED TENT BY A FOXHOLE. We had a crew of soldiers assigned to sandbag the FDC truck and each soldier was responsible for personal safety. I sandbagged my tent and had a foxhole right next to it. One night we took incoming rounds and I woke up in the foxhole without any memory of how I got there. The noise of incoming apparently alerted me, and without waking up I dove into the hole next to the tent and made it through the mortar attack without any problems. We lost our chief of section in this area and I was promoted to take his place. This was how promotions occurred in a combat zone.

off in a lidded kettle. I felt a tingling down in my toes, a vast shiver across my neck. I prayed it wasn't the start of an all-out Chinese offensive.

Just as quickly as it started, an uneasy calm descended. Men began moving. Orders were shouted over the quiet ground. I stood up out of the foxhole, realizing what had happened. Infiltrators?

I walked toward the ravine where the rounds had struck, my rifle at the ready. The medics were up ahead, trying to determine if there were any wounded. I hoped they wouldn't find any. I saw Sefton's tent, untouched. He was standing next it, wearing only a T-shirt and shorts. He waved as I approached, pointed to a smoking hole not 20

FDC TRUCK BEING SERVICED. Art Schwerin was our maintenance man assigned to make sure that the electrical generator was always ready to go because we had to have electric power for the lights, ventilation, and radios in the FDC truck. Art's assignment was from the wire/radio section, and he was very diligent at taking his job seriously.

feet away. I asked about Scheffer. He said Scheffer had taken off with a sergeant to check the perimeter where a couple of laundry boys got through during the night.

Sefton lit a cigarette. His hands were trembling. We sat down together and waited.

Scheffer and the sergeant came back about a half-hour later when the sun was crawling up. Scheffer came over to the tent. His voice was hollow. He said they had found two of the perimeter guards, killed in their sleeping bags, bayoneted.

Sefton hung his head. I felt a deep, clawing anguish deep in my stomach.

The infiltrators had set up a mortar right next to the dead guys.

173

Scheffer and the sergeant had killed them both, but not before they threw about seven rounds into our position.

Before the day was over we moved out of position with our guns, into the infantry group that was part of the search task force. It was a scary proposition. Whenever advancing forces created a bulge in the line, it opened them up to being cut off by a collapse in the line behind them. It made for uneasy going. The strategy, if you could call it that, was to locate the main body of the enemy and hold them off until the infantry cleaned out the areas on both flanks. It was a good idea when it worked right, but it made for uneasy sleep. For two nights I rolled and tossed, kept awake by the incessant small arms fire in the hills, the chatter of machine guns and the intermittent thud of a mortar round. It was better to be awake than be caught in your sack. We slept with our rifles.

A day of relative quiet followed. Wrote a letter while I was directing the 155 howitzers on a mortar position that had been harassing us for the past two nights. The infantry was busy trying to clear out the surrounding hills, to straighten out the line. The Chinese were masters at hiding in the hills, especially when the trees were in full bloom. They took advantage of every rock, every crevasse, every bush. We knew it would be a while before we attained superiority.

Bob Schranck came back from Japan. He had been in the military hospital in Osaka, recuperating from his wound. I talked to him briefly, was glad to see him in good shape. He was now 44 days behind me in rotation, which wasn't good for him.

I also had a chance to talk to the chaplain, who was new to division artillery. He generally stayed at division forward which was 15 to 20 miles back. This chaplain was different than most. He was diligent about getting to some outfit every Sunday, regardless of the weather or the danger. Unlike the former chaplain, this one actually took time to talk to me or anyone else who needed his word. He seemed genuinely interested in my background and my opinions. It was his first move out of division to the front lines but he impressed me as one who would not allow the enemy to thwart his work.

I was out on my feet. Lack of sleep, a good case of nerves, hazy vision and inadequate food had made me dead tired. The medics gave me some pills, told me to calm down and relax so I could get some sleep. The incoming stuff was new to me. Frazzled nerves and fear could often bring a man to his knees.

By the 4th, things were back to normal. I had a fair night's sleep. The infantry pushed forward on our part of the front and straightened out the line. The ROKs pulled back a bit. The 24th Regiment in front of us held in good shape despite the intensity of the firefight. In all we lost one man to incoming artillery fire and another FO out on the line.

Rain again, one of those punishing downpours. I had stripped down to my skivvies before crawling into the bag that night, had rolled my clothes up in a ball. Sometime during the storm, water came in, soaked my tent floor and everything on it, my clothes and billfold included. My sleeping bag was water resistant and was always on top of a piece of canvas I had acquired to protect it from the bottom up. But the rain was so hard it ran over the top of the canvas and soaked everything. The next morning I emptied my billfold, hung its contents out like laundry, waited for the rain to subside.

I was on standby that day. Bob and I had headsets on in division artillery, had our phones hooked together. Music was coming over the wire. I had bounced back with a good night's sleep. Slept again that afternoon. Started firing again at 16:00, right through to 22:30, laid 3,500 rounds into the enemy positions. The infantry advanced a mile and a half, across one mountain that rose 393 feet to 2,362 feet within a distance of 1,640 horizontal feet. Rugged going. Intense opposition. Some hills had to be bypassed. Never a good thing. I got off late, slept well until our usual 04:00 serenade. That's when the rounds started coming in again.

I was not on duty when the enemy rounds came in. I was asleep in my bag. Like before, the first startling whine of a shell awoke me like a slap on the face. It was close enough to shake my tent. I grabbed my boots and rifle and scampered outside, threw myself over the sandbags, landed in my six foot long, four foot deep hole as the second round came whistling in. Pelts of dirt rained in on top of me. My ears began ringing. Fear crawled up my legs. A moment later I heard the calls. "Medic! Medic!"

Someone had been hit. A Negro medic from Norfolk, Virginia, was the only one who ran toward the call. He had left his secure position and was racing toward the wounded man when I peered over the sandbags.

I heard someone shout, loud enough to hear that the chief of section had been hit.

I didn't hear any more rounds coming in. If they did, I ignored them. I dashed out toward the medic. Three other guys were there, leaning over a body. They had already lifted the SFC onto a stretcher. He was limp, no movement. He had taken shrapnel. The only wound I could see was a streak of blood across his forehead. The more severe one was deep beneath his jacket. The medic tore open his shirt, ripped open a sulfa pack, taped it to the deep purpled spot just above his stomach, told the nearest man to get an ambulance, quick. Another man lay close by. His name was Steve. He was a warrant officer. He had taken shrapnel in the foot. He stood up, groggy, but mobile. He limped away on one foot, behind the stretcher, supported by two other men.

Two other medics came up then. The colored boy from Norfolk glared at them, his eyes red with anger. He dressed the men down with the skill of a drill instructor, told them he was attending two wounded when they were laying in their holes, afraid to come out. They were both yellow, he said. He kicked at them, ordered them into the ambulance to get the SFC down to the field hospital.

I drifted back to my hole, laid there, waited for more explosions. No more came that morning. We had taken two rounds only. And one had to hit our section chief. As fate would have it, he had turned down rotation for a chance to go to Japan on R&R, to be with his Japanese girlfriend. They were about to set their wedding date. They had plans to return to the States, to start a family. He loved the woman. She was all he ever talked about.

The next day we were busy on the telephone, checking on the progress of the SFC and Steve. We learned that Steve would be all right. It was shortly after noon that the bad news came. Our chief had died. The mood in FDC was one of deep despair. It was the first time I had lost a close buddy, one of our own. It had a profound effect on me, a sorrow that wouldn't go away. I remembered the saying, *There, but for the grace of God, go I.* Death had knocked on our door and it had sickened me.

The nightly shelling, though terrifying, produced moments of humor as well. I usually took cover in my hole, between the sandbags. One night when scattered rounds were coming in I saw someone run past my hole, only to stop dead in his tracks. It was Frenchy. He seemed disoriented, unsure of where he was going. He was holding his boots in his hands, standing in his stocking feet. I asked him where he was going.

He looked down at me, blank-eyed, his face a mask of uncertainty, said he didn't know. He stammered incoherently, fear rising in his throat. I told him to get back to his hole before he got hit. Frenchy turned, looked at his boots as if to question why they were there. Then he turned and left.

Another sergeant was running for his own hole one night when he fell and skidded through the mud, right into the battalion commander's hole. He stayed there until the shelling was over. Two men in one hole, sardine fashion.

The next day I was sitting in front of the FDC truck writing a letter when I saw fire coming down the water trough from the freshwater spring. I didn't know what to make of it until I saw Schranck laughing his fool head off. He had been up to his old tricks. He had filled his helmet with gasoline, to clean his rifle. When he finished with the cleaning, he emptied the gasoline into the stream and lit it on fire. He thought it was the funniest thing he'd ever done. He was a good kid, a practical joker but sometimes I wondered if he used his head for anything but a hat rack.

We were busy with offensive fire plans against the enemy artillery pieces. The telephone was very busy all that day.

The weather was comfortable. The Chinese used it to good advantage, hiding their artillery pieces in the woods, using the leaves for cover. When they applied this tactic, they were able to move much closer than before. We pounded away at suspected locations, hoping that our FOs were correct in their sightings.

It was six months to the day since I landed in Korea. I still didn't have a firm date for my rotation.

By June 8 things had quieted down to near normal. I pulled my regular day shift and was out of the truck by afternoon. I got in some good sack time. That night I slept straight through, perhaps because

I learned that I would be the second enlisted reserve to rotate in the battery, the eighth in the battalion, subject to replacements arriving and being trained. I could live with that. It had a calming effect on my otherwise jittery existence. When I awoke the next morning I was bathed in sweat. The high temperatures and wet ground combined made for a brutal humidity. One could sweat standing still.

We moved out of mortar valley and back onto the main road, through the stately pines of King's Forest, the most beautiful area of Korea, in my estimation. We left the valley and ascended a narrow, winding road cut right through the hills. At the summit, we were in the clouds, close to the timberline. Rough, rugged terrain but extremely beautiful, a rolling, variegated patchwork of color, scented by the forest, a view that could sweep away a man's heart were it not for the war. As it was, I could only feel sorry for the infantry who had to penetrate that country on foot. I could understand why, at times, there were gaps in their lines.

We ended up close to the town of Chipori on the main north-south road from Seoul to Kumiva, a bit south and east of Chorwon, near Kumwa. The sector was called "The Chorwan Area" by the military.

Rotation was the main topic of conversation whenever a group assembled. Scuttlebutt had it that I would have to serve several months of inactive duty when I returned to the States. Did that mean living on an army post? I wasn't sure. I thought about the possibility of renting a trailer in St. Paul and pulling it to wherever I would be stationed. All I knew is that I had to be with Florence. I had more questions than answers. As always, I would just have to wait it out and see what happened.

Moved again the next day after a busy 18:00 to 20:00 shift. We dug in, were fortunate enough not to receive any incoming fire. The infantry in front of us was reporting limited resistance. For a change, we had a quiet day.

At 17:00 we received a radio message to dispatch someone by jeep to Kimpo Airfield, to pick up the battalion executive officer, because he had missed the plane from Japan. Kimpo was just outside Seoul, about 70 miles from our position. The fact that he was from Minneapolis excited my curiosity. I volunteered to ride shotgun with his regular driver. Our first stop was Service Battery. From there we were told to go to Kimpo and wait.

The ride to Kimpo was uneventful, but we were always alert for the unexpected. The jeep did not offer us a comfortable ride. It was not a pleasure vehicle. The roads were terrible, carved by mortar rounds, detoured around abandoned equipment, holes everywhere, made all the more ominous because we had to travel in blackout conditions. The front windshield was down on the hood. There was no top. The headlights were covered, except for a very narrow slit for illumination. We sat in metal bucket seats. I had the one in the rear. It was understood that when we picked up the major, I would ride in back with his duffel.

We arrived at Kimpo about 22:00. Four hours to travel 70 miles. The major was nowhere to be found. The officer in charge told us there would be two planes in the following morning. We were told to get some sleep in one of the shelters. It was there we found some litters and a couple of blankets. In the Air Force each person had a bed, a wooden floor, screened windows, a tent roof, much better facilities than the infantry or the FDC for that matter.

The morning dawned bright and sunny. Still no major. We went to the 25th division replacement depot to see if we could get breakfast. There we saw a herd of replacements coming in, new boys from the States. They looked much the same as we did that first day we set foot in Korea, confused, blank-faced, uncertain, scared. By now I could call myself a veteran, and I suppose I looked like one, skuffy and whiskered as I was.

The major's plane came in late that morning. He was a much younger man than I had expected but he had the polish of an experienced officer. He wasted little time on formality. I helped him get his things out of the plane, told him informally that I was from St. Paul, that I lived near the fairgrounds. We chatted briefly.

I was about to heave the duffel into the jeep when the major grabbed my arm. He informed me that his duffel was not just an ordinary clothes bag. It was also his liquor carrier. He winked. I got the message clearly. I settled the duffel into the back seat with the care of a valet. Then we headed back—another four hours on the road, but easier the second time because we were in daylight.

The R&R boys returned, filled with the Devil's brew. One of the boys in the section brought back 11 bottles of hooch. I wondered why they got so much pleasure out of drinking. They didn't try to hide it. They were loud, stumbling, hazy-eyed and vulgar. I hoped they'd sleep it off before resuming their duties. We needed clear heads on line, not a bunch of stewheads. It seemed that Kevin, our new radio chief, the radio operator and I were the only sober ones in the outfit.

On June 13 we moved a short distance north, behind the 27th Infantry. The line was straight again. We were on highway Number 3, a short distance from the town of Chipori, in a valley between two high ridges. The infantry was just outside Kumbwa. We dug in for a possible stay of one to ten days. It was a much-welcomed rest area after moving fast and often. We prepared for the long stay, bagged ourselves up real good, hoped it would stay quiet.

I wrote Florence that we had 57 enlisted reservists in the battalion when we arrived on December 7, 1950. For whatever the reasons, we now had 25 ERs in the battalion. The rotation plan at the time allowed for six men to go out with every quota, which would spread the rotation over five months. I was lucky. I was in the second group. The battalion commander had the final word on who would go. If he felt you were critical to his operation, he could hold you back. In other words, a trained replacement must be available in order for rotation to take place. I was in good shape. I figured I could leave as soon as July or as late as November. As usual, I wasn't sure. I could only hope for July. Naturally, the Regular Army boys were pissed off at the enlisted reserve rotation plan. They didn't appreciate the fact that we were here by recall and not because we enlisted, as they did.

Quiet for two days. It gave me a chance to clean up and get some sleep. I was busy during the 18:00 to 20:00 shift. I checked in all the night's shooting to division every morning, and had to bring the daily report up to date. It was usually the work of the duty officer but he generally passed it down, knowing it would be done correctly.

Before I had the report finished, the telephone rang. It was regimental liaison. They reported that the 25th Recon Company had captured two big mortars out in front of us. Those were the two that had been throwing things at us. Good news. We all breathed a sigh of relief knowing that we were a little safer in our sacks from that moment on.

Every battalion has two observation planes assigned to them for air observation posts (OPs). It was rare that we got to see the pilots we talked to on the radio. But one of the boys did come into FDC to talk to us. He was a great guy, about 25, sandy-haired. He told us he'd take us up sometime to see what it was like. He flew the same kind of Piper Cub that Florence's brother flew, except that the OP's was a two-passenger plane. I looked forward to a flight, knowing that it might never happen. The observer had more important things to do than fly soldiers over the front lines.

On the day Florence was graduating from the university, I stayed in my tent, out of the steady rain. In the afternoon I got a booster shot for typhus. It was the end of the shot program. I was in good shape for the next six months. I dozed late that day, imagining myself back home, watching Florence accept her diploma. It would be a proud day for her family, and mine. Congratulations and cake and celebration at the Whites' house. Instead of the laughter, I listened to the rain on my canvas. Instead of the cake, I ate a biscuit with jelly, a can of stew. But I was there in heart. I could almost hear her voice above the incessant chatter of the rain.

June 18. Quiet again. Waiting for the infantry to move.

I decided to draw out all the money I had coming to me, pay off Bob Schranck, and send the rest home by money order. I didn't want to take the chance of having the record group screw up if I happened to leave suddenly on rotation. I received a letter that was written on the 11th. Six days for passage. The fastest delivery yet, considering the number of post offices it had to clear. In the letter was a small picture packet. I must have studied it for an hour. It fit well into my pocket. I carried it with me wherever I went.

Very hot. We haven't fired a round in two days.

I got off at 14:00 and went with Stallard, Frenchy, Schranck and Little Joe to a small swimming hole a couple of miles from our location. It lay in the bowl of a creek, surrounded by trees, a deep, cool pool of water that reflected the sky, turned silver in the sunlight. It was a place often used by the Mama-sans, where they washed clothes.

Sometimes they bathed their children in the shallow water. None of the natives were there that day, just us guys. It was a peaceful area, away from the discord of camp. We cooled ourselves, dozed in the shade, talked very little, mentally transported ourselves back home through thoughts as deep as the water. Didn't hear a sound there, except the birds and the murmur of the creek through the reeds.

When we returned that night I had the watch. I was lucky enough to tune in some music over the telephone. Schranck was sleeping on the computer bench, his head nested in the crook of his arm, indicating that his eye had healed quite well. The latest issue of *Stars and Stripes* hinted that 50,000 men were on the way to Korea to rotate some of the troops. The article gave me added hope that I'd be home soon. Others said it was only intended to quiet wild rumors from back home, that the civilians were beginning to tire of the "police action" that was taking so many lives. Before the night was over I downed several more APC tablets to attack the pounding headache that came from nowhere. I hadn't taken any pills for a week. I hoped it wasn't the start of a recurring problem.

On June 20 I received a raise in pay. The first sergeant came to FDC in the morning and informed me that my promotion had come through. I was officially a sergeant, probably due to the fact that Captain Joe had continually raised concerns that my responsibility as chief of section didn't carry with it the suitable rank. The first sergeant, being Regular Army, did not have a tender spot in his heart for reservists. It was obvious when he told me about the promotion. He didn't favor the decision. But for me, it did mean more money and added privileges when rotation time rolled around. I was happy that someone finally recognized my importance in FDC. To top it off, we received 16 new men that day and three were assigned to FDC. That meant I might no longer be classified as essential. By my calculations, rotation would occur sometime at the end of July or early August. I was on cloud nine that day. Only a month and a half to go. Then I could kiss the war goodbye.

Another quiet day. We didn't fire a single round. I was on from 06:00 to 08:00 to prepare the morning report and call division to inform them of the night's activity or lack thereof. The infantry had repelled a very small attack but even that required paperwork.

The next night was different. The telephone rang about 20:00, then continually until midnight. It was our first night without a moon, and true to form the Chinese used cover of darkness to harass our front line. They hit one company hard. We fired back, even harder, stopped them in their tracks. Then came an air warning. Bedcheck Charlie was in the vicinity. I finally hit the sack about 03:00, slept until morning. Awoke in a sweat. Hustled to get my last minute letter to the post office. Got my mail in just before breakfast.

We learned that the 25th Division was going into reserve but not their artillery. We were ordered to move and support the 9th ROK Division. They had foot soldiers but no artillery. Then came the worrisome part. We hoped they wouldn't fold in front of us in the face of an attack, as had happened several times before to other artillery outfits. The lower the ROK division number, the more experience they had in the field. High number, new outfit. We hoped the 9th was an old division but no one knew for sure.

Quiet days were lazy days. The more time I had on my hands, the more I wasted. We were busiest at night. From 22:30 to 01:30 we played hide and seek with Bedcheck Charlie. He came around, following one of our planes that had dropped flares in and around the area to keep the FOs alert. He used the light to toss out his grenades. He didn't hit anyone or even come close but he had us in our holes a couple of times. He unloads, goes back to his base, comes back again. We all hoped that someday we'd shoot him down. Things were better when we didn't have to sweat him out.

The weather is still hot. My skin was deeply tanned.

I laughed at Stallard. He was a small guy, weighed about 135 pounds, was five-ten in height. We always joked, whenever he took a bath, that he'd have to fight the current. Aside from a strong wind, he did just fine, except for the clothes he wore. Most of his shirts were so big they looked like sacks on his body. Others were too tight. Nothing was standard in the Army. Stallard always seemed to get the odd fits. There were days he looked like a circus clown. I, on the other hand, weighed in at about 230. I could cram into a size 36 or fight my way into a size 34. Larger sizes weren't always available. There were days I looked to be the opposite of Stallard.

It was late in the afternoon when Captain Joe called me into his tent. I remember it as being hot inside, as it was during those lazy days when I camped with the Boy Scouts on the Saint Croix River north of Stillwater, the smell of warm canvas like an intoxicant, the air thick with heat. He was sitting in his chair next to a small collapsible desk. His shirtsleeves were rolled up above his elbows, his collar unbuttoned, freely exhibiting the coarse black hair high on his chest. He responded to my brief salute, motioned me to the second chair, then leaned forward. It was evident he had something important to say. His eyes were directed straight at mine, like point-blank artillery fire. I seized up temporarily, until he spoke. He asked me straight out if I had ever considered making the Regular Army a career.

I stiffened. It was not the message I had expected. I caught the slight nod of the captain's head as he indicated his desire for a positive reply.

My reply was negative. I told him I wanted to go back home as soon as possible.

The captain leaned back in his chair, wiped a bead of sweat from his temple, said he understood, with a wife back home, my being a newlywed. He asked what I'd be doing in civilian life.

My tension evaporated under the softness of his voice. He was a different Captain Joe than the one who occasionally barked orders. He seemed more relaxed, content in the heat, almost like a father giving a son sound advice.

I told him I was going back to work with my father in his refrigeration company, that he wants me to learn the business so I could take it over some day.

The captain nodded. Then he rubbed his lips as if to pull the words away from his mouth. His offer was simple. What if the Army offered me the chance to become an operations sergeant? I'd be out of FDC, away from the fighting, training other men, with an excellent chance for promotion when rotation came. I'd be stationed in the States. My wife could be with me. Everything I'd need in a nice neat bundle.

I didn't answer straight out. Rather, the offer took me quite by surprise. I swallowed my words thoughtfully and as I pondered the possibility he continued by saying that I was a dedicated soldier, who didn't get drunk off duty, didn't squander my money or get wrapped up in questionable diversions. I had a good record. My Form 21 (Active Service Record) implied that I was highly qualified. I had received several outstanding reports. All combined, it would put me in good standing for artillery school or some other related area.

I folded and unfolded my hands, rubbed my fingers together in an instant of nervous tension. Nothing he could say would deter me from returning home to civilian life, yet his offer was intriguing. It did offer an opportunity, but nothing to compare with the future I might have with my father. Besides, Florence was a homebound girl. She wouldn't want to hop, skip, and jump across the country as the wife of a serviceman. And, though a position in artillery school would be attractive, there would soon be other wars to fight, perhaps even more vicious and brutal than Korea. It was the one thing the captain failed to mention.

I told him my mind was made up. I wanted to return home.

Captain Joe nodded; leaned back in his chair. His eyes traveled around the tent, perhaps to spots where many of his own memories were stored. He was Regular Army, on his way to becoming a major. He was committed to the service. I was a cut-and-dried civilian who happened to wear sergeant's stripes.

He told me that the Army has been good to him. I, too, could find a permanent home in the service. I could be practically guaranteed the rank of lieutenant once I was out of artillery school. Again, he said I'd make a good officer, even though I sometimes squalled at Army regulations.

I snickered, told him I wouldn't fit. Squalling was my nature.

He raised his hand, said the Army needed good squealers, someone who could see the problems and set them straight. Again, I refused.

He made one last stab at convincing me, asked if I would be willing to stay until the last bunch of reservists went home. If I did, he'd see that I was rated to master sergeant.

I shook my head in a slow, negative response. I wanted to go home.

He leaned back and slapped his knees, wiped the sweat back from his forehead, cocked his head and said that at least he'd tried. Everyone has their own agenda.

I nodded.

He stood up, tried to brush the wrinkles out of his shirt, mentioned something about protecting our freedom, that we couldn't let those bastards get the best of us.

Then he glared at me, not in anger, but with an urgency that might compel a less determined man to change his mind. I stood up and faced him and saw in his eyes a deeper, more imposing, sentiment one did not see at a distance. He was, after all, a human being, with a terrible job to do, so the rest of us could go back home to live our lives in peace. It was at that moment that my appreciation for all the Captain Joes in the world reached a new level of respect.

He followed me out of the tent. We stood for a moment in the sunlight, watching the soldiers nearby, heard a muffled roar somewhere over the hills. He put a hand on my shoulder, told me to have a good life, to give my wife a big hug for him.

I walked back to my pup tent, crawled inside, into the profound heat, found release from my tension, tingled then with the unbound realization that I would soon be going home. And in that canvas sheath, alone with my thought, I prayed that nothing would happen to change that wonderful and hopeful probability.

15

THE LAST MILES

At the end of June I was busy working with two draftees, trying to break them in on FDC. They had no idea of what they were training to do. We were in reserve and not firing. The training was more classroom instruction than actual combat experience, although they did get to fire one mission.

We had received 120 replacements during the month. It meant that a good number of men would be rotated. I tried to pump Major Karl on when I would go but he did not give me a direct answer. Perhaps he was tired of my persistent questioning. I knew I was near the top of the list but that didn't seem to mean much.

Mac, the medic, left on June 26. He had arrived in Korea the same day I did. He was going home under the Division Artillery medics' quota. He was the only one.

I went back to Service Battery and played softball again. We won 4 to 3. They had the equipment necessary to level off the field. They had a near-perfect diamond, except for grass. We went swimming afterwards in a big body of water. I was out in the sun all afternoon without a shirt. No burn. With all the past exposure, my skin had become burn proof.

No noise, except for the occasional bark of the big guns.

We were supporting the 9th ROK again and living in a new area. We erected a small wall-tent for six occupants, crowded but semi comfortable. I made a bed out of ten ammo boxes and an air mattress. It kept me off the ground. Mosquito netting discouraged the flies. We had roll-up canvas sides for good ventilation. Cool nights. Good sleeping.

Not much going on, except straightening out in the CP. We worked mostly at night, with five new men pulling FDC shifts. We allowed them to do as much as possible, to train them quickly. They had learned fundamentals well but needed practice. They were nearly ready to take over.

The sergeant major in charge of rotation came into the truck and told me our ER rotation remained unchanged, veterans first, those with previous service second. That would put me into the second slot. If that rule held up, I was convinced I'd be out by November 30 or earlier, depending on the number of replacements that were coming in steadily. Dreams on which to build a future.

On July 1 we received a written notice from Division Artillery with instructions to read it every 15 minutes on open radio. The message was clear, concise and hopeful. It read, in effect:

"The United Nation's forces have received word that the North Korean and Chinese leaders would like to meet on neutral ground to begin direct and formal discussions intended to bring this struggle to a close. Our government has responded affirmatively and has told the opposing forces that we are ready to meet them at a location of their choice. We are now awaiting a direct response. Although this news will affect each and every element of our Armed Forces, we urge you to remain alert and strong in your resolve not to diminish your readiness for battle. It is essential that we meet this offer hopefully but with caution and allow the peace overture to take its course."

The communiqué was good news, but it had little effect on anyone in our unit, other than as a topic of discussion. We didn't trust the Chinese. For all we knew, it was a ploy. Our forward observers were given the word to be extremely alert to any enemy movements. And so we waited.

I was off the next day. I slept most of the afternoon. In the evening I played ball against Charlie Company. It was a game that would have challenged the pros. We beat them 9 to 8 in extra innings. Although it was generally hot during the day, the evenings were cool. Conditions were perfect for the game. Afterwards Schef and I went down to the creek, sat with our feet in the water. Someone had dammed it up so the water was knee deep.

On payday my account swelled to $396. I drew my account clean and paid Bob the $25 I owed him, sent a money order to Florence in the amount of $350. The final adjustment to my change in grade would come next time and would amount to about $1 per day.

On the 7th of July we sent a gun battery forward to get into range. They pulled back that same night. Nothing doing on the front. Perhaps the Chinese were sincere about wanting to discuss peace terms.

The next day Stallard, Schranck, Scheffer and I received word that we were going to teach FDC classes to the replacements, which would include actual computations to the gun batteries, radio and telephone procedures. We would hold the classes in the big tents and in the FDC truck, depending on the number of men involved and the event at hand. Ron Scheffer was a trained teacher. He helped set up the classes. The only problem was, Scheffer had never talked on any kind of radio. That part he left up to the rest of us. All in all, we had about seven men to break in. The timing and location of our guns was perfect. The gun crews would also be training their telephone operators in mock missions.

Peace rumors kept coming at a furious pace. Additional communiqués indicated a definite desire for talks. We could feel the almost electric tension in the air. Everyone walked with a lighter step. Some began whistling again. Even the sun appeared brighter. Peace, of course, would be the answer to many prayers, including my own. They said the date to watch was the 10th or 15th of July.

Rotation was constantly on my mind. We learned that on the 12th, Pop and a sergeant would go home. Both had World War II experience and were close to 30 years old. We were happy for them. Their departure would leave eight enlisted reserves in the battery, without any World War II vets remaining. I wrote Florence that if she could find an apartment available on September 1st to take it. I was that sure I'd be home by them. I was beginning to tingle with anticipation.

We had our first in-tent class with the replacements. It went extremely well, considering their lack of experience and our first try at teaching. We were confident we could teach them well enough so they could handle real fire missions when they came in.

We played the 159th Battalion with a combined team from the "A," "C" and Headquarters Battery. It was a great game. We won 8 to 1. They got only three hits. We were very consistent.

Later, after dark, I played cards again. I started with two one-dollar bills, which I would either lose or multiply. Luckily the money multiplied. More to send home. I figured our account would be close to $1000 when I returned home. It would be enough to give Florence and me a good start, even if it was at the Leamington Hotel in Minneapolis.

Didn't do much of anything on the 4th. I worked out the bumps and bruises from the ball game and boiled some clothes in order to have something clean to wear. I wrote home, told Florence to cut back on the boxes of goodies, to limit them to animal crackers, which all of the boys liked.

Just when I thought I had everything figured out, the impossible happened. One of the new boys who was working the telephone got tired, and without notifying anyone walked off the job. That could have been very dangerous, had the Chinese decided to kiss off the peace talks. It would have left our forward elements extremely vulnerable. I was the new chief of section at the time and I went directly to Captain Joe who blew up over the situation. The slacker would no doubt get the book thrown at him, for abandoning his duty station. I never saw him again.

I attempted to send a money order home to Florence. The paymaster had just cleared the books. Everyone was up to date, paid in full before the start of a new fiscal year. I didn't draw any money, just wanted to make a money order application. It didn't go through because I failed to include my serial number (US-57-504-587). Army red tape. Another delay. Frustration again.

Classes started at 08:30 and ran to 10:30 each day. We were intent on training our replacements fast, so that when the 25th came back on line they would be able to take over. It would also free Stallard and me when our rotation dates arrived. Four of our students were from the Southern hills, slow moving, with the pace of a mule. They weren't dumb, just slow to learn, talk and act, as if learning was a chore they needn't do before sundown. It was imperative that they learn to work fast, finger-snapping fast. When information came into FDC to change deflection settings right or left, along with elevations for the guns, it had to be done in a matter of seconds, not before the sun went down. We tried to hammer this into them and all we got in return was a slow drawl that usually ended in, "Yea, sergeant, we done got it." We figured, once the firing started and the hair on their necks bristled and their hearts started pumping with the fury of an air compressor, they'd hurry. Damn right they'd hurry.

By the second week in July I was beginning to feel sorry for myself. I was on pills again, to settle my nerves. My headaches were frequent, pounding at the base of my skull. My eyes were sore. I was beginning to hate the country, the brambled hills, the steaming valleys, the incessant flies that played with my sanity. Were it not for softball and a new volleyball net, I would have fallen into a mood of despair. Thank God for the athletic reprieves. I didn't like it when I got mean, snarly and unpleasant to be with. Sometimes I disliked myself for becoming a victim to the damn insanity of war.

The Korean cooks we had didn't help my frustration. They were the most ignorant people I have ever met. None of them spoke English. They pointed at things, mumbled words we couldn't understand, often failed to get their message across. The GIs were not patient with them and even an occasional slap on the face from a nervous GI didn't seem to faze them. They just glared back and did what they were instructed to do, serve food, serve it fast and serve it abundantly. The Koreans got three square meals a day, just as we did. Their presence meant that no GI had to work KP. They did all the cleaning, all the cooking. Occasionally they gave out under the strain. I saw one Korean collapse. His legs just failed to hold him up. Fatigue? Sickness? We wondered sometimes if the food was contaminated.

We had movies almost every night. I did not sit through a single one, start to end. My nerves were wearing thin, to the point where I had trouble controlling my emotions. I paced some of the night hours along the edge of our camp, trying to calm myself down in the silence of my foreign world. My new job was part of it, a responsibility I could do without. As chief of section I was open to all kinds of verbal shots from the men, who gave them without thought, as if I were a target for their wrath, their confusion, their indignity. They would just as soon swear at me as look at me and they cursed with regularity. My letters to Florence were beginning to ramble. I had nothing new to say. My complaints were scribbled on paper, sent home to the only available ear.

Peace talks at Kaesong were about to get underway. Guarded news from Armed Forces radio came over our lines daily. But fighting still raged, for whatever the reason, another gained yard, another chunk of worthless ground, another shattered tree to claim, another foot of scorched earth to put under the boot. It seemed so senseless, wasting lives while others contemplated peace. The absurdity of war. Our unit, back in reserve, bored out of our heads. Men dying on the front while we played baseball. It made me feel absolutely useless at times. Rumors of a cease-fire became rampant. Talk. Talk. Talk. To top it all off, a tank took out all of our telephone lines. We were unable to communicate with anyone.

July 9: overcast sky, intermittent rain, gray and dismal. I was routed out at 06:00 for garrison duty. Had to remain busy until noon. We played several games of volleyball in the afternoon, to loosen up, to stay active.

In the evening we played the 159th again, minus our good pitcher. We picked up a replacement from "A" Battery, a kid we called "Coop." He did all right. We won 8 to 4. Both teams played hard. The colored boys were fun to play with. They were all rhythm, as if they were propelled by interior motors. The game ended in rain. The constant swirl of dust finally settled down. Days before we had drained the nearby rice paddy, so the mosquito population had dwindled.

The big H-Washon reservoir was east of us. We had plenty of water and good PX rations. We received hair tonic, shaving equipment and Coca-Cola from supply. I drank a can of beer now and then.

On July 10, negotiations began in Kaesong, in Panmunjom Province. We knew it would be some time until they reached an accord, if ever. Until then, more men would die.

I was up at 06:30. We started a training program complete with every essential item. Classes lasted for over four hours. I could not understand why they started so early. I spent the afternoon in my tent, napping. We lost another man to rotation, a radio operator named Bob who lived in a small Wisconsin town. He pitched for the Battery team. Now we would have to find a new thrower.

Problems again with my teeth. Despite the fact that I brushed regularly, we still lacked fresh vegetables. The cooks did the best they could with what they had. Cans provided food but not some of our essential vitamins. They said diet had a lot to do with our teeth problems. Toothaches and headaches kept me awake during the night. The next day I hooked a ride with the messenger and went back to the dentist.

David, the dental assistant I had shipped over with, had rotated. The dental staff was working shorthanded. When I finally did get into the chair, the dentist found a quarter inch hole deep in my first molar on the right side. It had to go. After the Novocain, he pulled and yanked, and when he put a clamp on the tooth, it shattered. It must have been rotten. The dentist said I was entitled to a bridge when I returned to the States. He said it might take six months for the record to get to the VA, that they would notify me. I finished just before chow time and hooked a ride back, but only after talking to the athletic officer to put a plug in for our baseball team. He promised me he would try and arrange as many games as possible by putting a notice in the daily information sheet.

When I returned to camp I found that two trucks and many jeeps were loading up to go to the Jack Benny show. I jumped in with Bob Schranck and we rode over an hour on a dusty, winding road, 20 to 30 miles, to the rear and south of our position. I rode in the back of the truck. Officers rode in the jeeps. We arrived about an hour and 15 minutes before the show started. We both got a good seat about 30 feet from the stage. We were seated on the ground, in a giant semicircle. We used our helmets for seats. It kept us off the damp, dirty ground. Sitting on helmets was not comfortable, but it was standard practice, although the officers took a dim view of it because it often dented the helmets. The Koreans had the ability to squat with both feet flat on the ground, with their butts about 2 or 3 inches between them and the earth. They could sit like that for hours, straight-backed, smoking either a pipe or cigarettes. Whenever you saw two or three in a group, they were all seated in that standard position. We could never sit like that.

Jack Benny put on one helluva show. He had Errol Flynn with him, Marjorie Reynolds, and an accordion player who stole the show. She was on stage most of the time, and had very little pancake makeup on compared to the others. She was a grand American girl and the 3,000 to 4,000 boys really whooped it up. The show was wonderful. Those people deserved all the thanks in the world.

We got back about 21:00. I cleaned up and hit the sack. It was my night off.

The next day we had a softball game with Service Battery. They had beaten "C" Battery and wanted a shot at us. We trounced them 15 to 4. The game really cost them. It was a known fact that some of the gambling personnel from Service Battery were betting against us. Some of the boys had as much as $150 bet on the game.

Moved again on the 15th, with the gun batteries, fired again at the Chinese, were once again rationed to 15 rounds per day, per howitzer.

Shifted again. Had all of two hours sleep the entire day. I was about to put up my tent when the officers informed us that all enlisted men had to be in foxholes. We bitched, dug. The ground was soft. I carved myself a good spot. I wasn't much for sleeping in a hole, so I went out behind a hill and pitched two ponchos over some bushes next to a dike. I slept there until morning.

Things were quiet the next day. The tanks had once again ripped up our wire.

The rotation list had me to the top bracket for Headquarters Battery. Arky and Paul left. They were the last of the World War II vets in the outfit. There were now four on the next rotation shipment: Bob Schranck, Pat, Puff, and me. Bob would probably leave first because of his eye.

Moved again on the 17th. The day started at 05:30, ended at 22:00 after we dug in. The 1st Cavalry had holes, but everyone insisted on putting sandbags around the sides higher than the truck. As usual, the base wasn't wide enough. When it got too high it toppled. Bob was on top of the stack putting on bags, catching bags from one of the new men, when it fell. Bob jumped clear, but Jack was buried beneath the bags. We hustled to get the bags off him. He was okay except for some bad bumps and bruises. He insisted he was okay, so we didn't call the medics. The next day, however, he was so sore he could hardly walk. Live and learn.

Word came: Bob Schranck would go home on the 21st. We did

some firing the next day, but worked on our fortress most of the time. We had sandbags up the sides and were about to put a log roof over the top. The 82nd Field Artillery Battery of the 1st Cavalry Division was supporting us. They had built an amphitheater with ammo boxes for seats. It was a large construction job. Frenchy and I went to a movie there. It was a pleasure, not having to sit on one's helmet. The movie was *Lullaby of Broadway* with Doris Day. It was a good show.

On the 19th, the negotiators at Panmunjom reached an agreement and began work on the task of drawing up boundaries for the demilitarized zone. It was welcome news. But it seemed the Chinese didn't get the word. The very next day they started to come through toward the 27th Infantry. We fired everything we had at them. More dead, while others awaited signatures on paper.

Rained again. Most of the fellows were not as fortunate as I was. I was in a small wall tent with ammo boxes for a bedstead, high and dry. I had a couple of inches of water on the floor but it didn't bother me. The water ran under the tent. Later, we built up sandbagged walls again but they fell. We hoped the new people would learn something from the routine rain exercise.

It was so wet the next day that we moved Headquarters Battery to a new spot. It was on a dry riverbed, good ground, except that the water rose about two feet after we had pitched our tents. We adjusted. We also found a place close by where we could bathe every morning, only three feet deep in the middle but nice and cool.

Bob Schranck left on the 22nd. He was all smiles, on his way home. He said he might have to hold up at a hospital in Japan for a few days, to check his eye. I was happy for him. We shared an embrace.

Hot weather set in. Muggy. Scorching heat.

It rained for a couple of days, so hard we had to move. The water in the creek had receded, but now it was up again and threatening our position.

We were very busy in FDC with our new men. It was a problem getting the fire out fast and accurate. They were learning by doing, critical stuff, to keep the fanatic Chinese at bay. One was an ex-cop from Los Angeles, the other a former honor guardsman for

General MacArthur. They had both operated radios, so it was easy to put them to work. One other fellow, a married draftee with one child, was eager to get ahead. He had a good attitude. He'd make a good FDC man.

I acquired another ammo box and a mosquito bar. I hoped we would stay in our present position, close to the water. We had a big tent near the shoreline. The flies were out in abundance.

My new rank had its privileges. Most of the troops were up at 06:15 and had work details every day. I rested most of the time, cleaned my weapons in case the battery commander came around and wanted to check it out. The truck was cramped, beastly hot, with poor ventilation. The lights were fine, but only added to the heat.

Sefton and I were called out of the movie one evening just after it started. Once again we fired off many rounds until the Chinese settled down. The temperature in the truck must have been 120 degrees F. Damn those Chinese. Didn't they know peace talks were underway?

On the 26th I received my first concrete clue that I was nearing rotation. I had not taken R&R, so my golden day was coming fast. The only unknown was how many would go in the next quota and when. We also received a new commanding officer and a new first sergeant, but that was of little importance to the much larger picture.

Had a pleasant surprise. A three quarter ton truck stopped by and Ron stepped out. He had been with me on the ride over from the States to Japan, and was now stationed just across the 38th parallel, in reserve. He had taken 24 hours off and had decided to look me up. We had a good visit. I took a survey jeep and drove him back. I didn't stay long. I had the responsibility to watch the chow line that night.

I was on duty from 01:30 to 04:00. I slept on the computer table the entire time. It was finally quiet on the line.

The next day, the 27th of July, was tense. We were awaiting word from Kaesong. We knew the negotiators had agreed on all details of the armistice and were just waiting to sign the papers. Captain Joe came to work that morning a little under the weather, probably from his private celebration. He commented that he had put me in for sergeant first class. That was fine with me. It meant I would get another pay raise.

I walked down along the river, out where I was alone. Quiet there. No sounds of war that day, only the slow movement of the water. I prayed there wouldn't be any complications at the peace table, that we could finally turn our backs on the conflict, that no more men on either side would die simply for political gain. The breeze was sweet that day, a summer scent of grass and earth, dampened by the rain. I spoke to Florence, there, alongside the bank, told her I would write that "Golden Letter." I tingled at the thought that the war would soon be over, that I would be flying home, that I would again be in her arms.

Time moved so slow that afternoon, so very slow. Then it happened. At 10:00 hours on the 27th of July, General Harrison, the senior United Nations delegate, signed the armistice papers, as did the enemy delegate, General Nam Il.

Twelve hours later, at 22:00, the guns fell silent. Peace had come to Korea.

Ironically, our army estimated that the Chinese had lost over 72,000 men during the month of July, more than 25,000 of those killed in action. What a waste. Peace talks and death, hand in hand, as if one was impossible without the other. And how many of our boys had died? We didn't know or weren't told. But now it was over. Both sides could weep for their dead.

I was alone again that night, in my pup tent, looking at a picture of Florence in the glow of my flashlight. Never had anyone looked so beautiful. Deep inside, I felt a satisfying release of tension, a draining of my emotions. Outside I heard the pop, pop, pop, of small arms fire. Celebrations in the making. Whoops came across the ground from the medic tents. No more wounded. No more dead. The ambulances would cease their runs. The doors of the FDC would close. Hard to believe. I tried to write a letter that night, in the remaining heat of a 100-degree day, but the blue ink ran so much I couldn't read it. Instead, I laid the letter aside and slept.

We didn't do much the next day except get ready for the division move, which would take place the following day at 06:15. We were moving back to the same place as before, by another river.

Replacements came in: 18 for our battalion, 2 for Headquarters Battery, 16 for the guns. We were busiest during the hottest hours.

I received word on the 31st at 18:50 that I was going to Service Battery the following morning and that I would be at the replacement depot on August 2. Four were going from HQ Battery, of which two were enlisted reservists.

On that day I wrote my Golden Letter. I told Florence to put the fountain pen away and start looking for an apartment. I would be home in a month.

I had never been so happy or nervous. It struck me all at once, a giddy feeling, a wringing of my senses. I breathed easier, moved at a faster pace, forgot about the heat. My mind raced ahead of me, to the truck, to the airport, to the flight, to the crossing. I was way ahead of myself, embraced in euphoria. All I wanted to do was laugh or cheer. I thought the smile on my face would be fixed there forever. I packed my belongings.

Kevin and I went back to check the mail when it started raining. The sky opened up in a farewell deluge. We were caught in the downpour. With it came a cold front, shoving the heat aside with a wet hand. It was the hardest rain we'd had for some time. Sheets of unending water turned the river into a cascade. I went back to my tent, crawled in, tied up all my letters. I intended mailing them back to Florence with a box of Bob Schranck's belongings. We waited out the rain. I tried to stay high and dry above my ammunition boxes. My foxhole filled with water.

I hoped my records wouldn't be fouled up going through processing. It was always a worry that something would go wrong, that my papers would be lost or misplaced. With thousands of men on the move, it made for a nervous wait.

My group arrived at the Young-Dong-Po replacement depot at 07:30 on August 2. I started out right away to get on the roster for pay, records and clothing forms. At the clothing issue station, we stripped, tossed out combat clothes in a pile to be burned. Then we walked to a delousing station where we were dusted and given new underwear. They kept us very busy.

We left for Inchon the following morning at 04:45. It began with a two-mile walk to the railroad station. From there we boarded a train, much better than the one we had taken inland on the day of our arrival. This one moved continually, no stopping. At Inchon, we would spend one to seven days before leaving for Sasebo, Japan. From there it would be one to nine days before I would board a ship for the United States.

We boarded an old ship, the *General Black*, once used in World War II to transport German prisoners of war. All the instructions on the bulkheads were written in German. We did not have soft water showers. The food tables were at standup height. I had no idea where the crew came from. Many were civilians. It was a filthy boat, made even worse by the slow passage.

We went ashore at Sasebo, in a harbor surrounded by mountains, traveled by bus to the army camp, which had been changed from an occupation unit to a replacement, transfer station. The buildings were clean, a wonderful change from the dirt and mud of the Korean battlefront. They kept us extremely busy with rules and regulations. All script had to be turned in. I sent all my money home via money order. They only allowed me to keep $25, which would discourage the temptation to gamble. Poker games and crap games were not allowed. There was no need for money. We didn't have to purchase anything.

As I was waiting in the block long lines, I sometimes could not believe I was going home. No matter who I was with, the conversation was always the same. Where are you going? What are you going to do when you get there? Pictures of girlfriends, wives, children, depending on their marital status. Grins. Calls of "hurry up, we gotta get home." I had one suit of new fatigues to my name. That was all. Showers. Sheets on my bed. A small touch of civilian life to ease the transition from war to peace.

They fed us well. We had a big steak dinner with all the trimmings.

My records were all up to date. I had been officially promoted to sergeant first class.

It was rumored that we'd leave for the States within two days. For once the rumor was correct. We boarded the huge troop ship that Sunday, thousands of us, with our hearts in our throats. I didn't even look back at Japan as we sailed out of the harbor entrance over the submarine nets. I looked at the ocean, eastward, to where the days would click off with infinite slowness, 14 in all.

Besides my countless hours on deck, my many hours in the sack, I did nothing. My rank of SFC kept me free of any duty responsibilities. I was a traveler with only one purpose.

The highlight of the voyage was an accidental meeting with William Best, the older brother of Donna Best, a classmate of ours from Murray High School. William and I did a lot of visiting, reminiscing, future planning, while traveling to California. We talked very little about the war, which seemed to fade with each passing mile.

I only had two nightmares on the troop ship. Others had more. It was not uncommon for someone to scream during the night.

We gathered at the rails to watch the good old U.S.A. form on the horizon, the mountains, the shoreline, the islands, the small watercraft speeding by, people waving, shouting. On the pier the band played again, "Stars and Stripes Forever," "When Johnny Comes Marching Home." It was thrilling to touch foot again on our land, to feel freedom alive in the air, to grasp that invisible sense of belonging that quickened the heart.

At Fort Lewis we had supper, then went to the PX to have our insignias sewed on our uniforms. We bedded down on mattresses. None of us, to the man, could wait for the sunrise.

In the morning a corporal came pounding in through the door. His voice was loud. "Reveille! Reveille! Hit the deck!"

The guy nearest him threw a pillow in his direction, cursed, told him we weren't recruits, that we just came back from Korea. The corporal glanced at our uniforms. All were sewn with sergeant stripes. He backed away from the catcalls. Sometime later a lieutenant came in and rousted us out.

The processing went smoothly. After the normal physical exams and paperwork, the day of release was announced. During the processing period I became aware of the possibility of flying a charter airplane from Seattle/Tacoma to Minneapolis for about one-half the cost of riding a scheduled airliner. The cost in 1951 for an airline coach ticket was about $100. If I could fall in with a specified number of men going into the Twin Cities, I could fly the charter for

$50. I checked around and found more than enough men who wanted to share the arrangement. I told the broker. He agreed to furnish a bus from Fort Lewis to the airport near Seattle, a field shared by the general airport and the Boeing Aircraft Company, a single strip, a small building for a terminal. We were to pay our fare when we entered the bus. We had cash, because we had all received our mustering out pay and mileage allowance to Minneapolis.

I was excited and anxious. I called Florence.

The bus and the broker arrived as promised and we all paid the broker as we boarded the bus. The first sign of trouble appeared when the bus stopped just outside the fort at a local bank and the broker deposited the funds. I didn't know at the time if that was standard procedure.

When we arrived at Boeing Field it was announced that our plane would be late, well beyond its intended arrival time of mid-afternoon. Many of the men were visibly angry. Some had been drinking. I stayed close to the broker. As the delays mounted, the men got increasingly harder to handle. I found an MP and told him our troubles. He immediately took the broker aside and told him in no uncertain terms that if the plane didn't arrive soon, he'd have to refund that money. And he'd be right there to make sure he did.

The broker shrugged, said the money was in the bank. The MPs look said it all. Then he sneered, told him to get the money or we'd have his ass. We were veterans, fighting a war in Korea and now we wanted to get home. He said if we didn't get our plane soon he'd turn his back for a minute and let us take our revenge.

Luckily, the charter airplane arrived at 23:00. Before it touched down the crash trucks were called into service because the plane reported that it had no brakes. This was more than the men could take. Repairs would take hours, perhaps days. We asked for and received our money back. Then we had to make arrangements to Minneapolis and quick. Our families had already been notified that we were going to fly. I sent a Western Union Telegram to Florence, informing her of the change.

I made arrangements to leave the next morning on a Northwest Airline flight at 06:00, but the airport was socked in by fog. Another delay. We had to wait until the fog cleared. Our arrival time was postponed until mid-afternoon.

We flew out of Seattle at the same time the charter flight left. I had a window seat on the way back, spent most of the time looking at the land below, the mountains, the rivers, the plains, clouds and clear sky, watching the miles drift by. I drank several cups of coffee. The guy next to me slept most of the way. We didn't talk much.

Minnesota was green. I knew it was Minnesota because of the lakes, the blue-white gems of water set amid the fields and the forests. My heartbeat quickened then. I could feel the glow inside, warming my shoulders. Then the announcement. We would be landing in ten minutes. We dropped out of the clouds, above that spread of river that could only be the Mississippi. My adrenaline was pumping. I could hardly swallow. Farms now. Buildings. The land coming up to greet me.

Touchdown.

The plane taxied to a place off the tarmac. I waited for unloading steps to be positioned by the door. We crowded the single aisle, eager, voices raised in celebration. The fresh air came in, bringing with it the smell of Minnesota.

My eyes were blurred when I saw my wife, Florence, my parents, sisters, aunts and uncles. Embraces were long, hard, and tender, the words like music.

It was over.

I was home again, that mid-afternoon of August 25, 1951.

On Saturday, August 25, 1951, the *St. Paul Dispatch* wrote the following:

11 St. Paul Vets Due in Seattle today.

Nine St. Paulites and two North St. Paul veterans are among the 2,849 rotation combat troops from the Korean War Zone scheduled to arrive in Seattle today. According to the Associated Press, the men are aboard the S. S. *Phoenix*. The St. Paulites on the passenger list are: Cpl. William Best, 1262 Raymond Ave.; Cpl. David T. Fay, 273 Central Ave.; Sgt. Raymond Fritzke, 472 Wabasha St.; Cpl. Curtice C. Hardenbrook, 1954

Country Rd. C.; SFC James W. Hawkland, 59-B Fort Snelling; SFC Richard B. Holmsten, 1512 Raymond Ave.; Cpl. Arthur A Kadlec, 2259-1/2 E. Minnehaha Ave.; Sgt. Charles E. King, 727 Dayton Ave.; SFC Russel P. Shifsky, 702 Edmond Ave.

The two from North St. Paul, Sgt. Keith R. Kingsley, 28 Castle Ave.; and Sgt. William E. McMahon, Jr.

We were civilians again.

INDEX